Sam Pulitzer
The Premise of a Better Life

Kunsthaus Glarus
After 8 Books

Foreword

"Can you afford yourself?" "Are you waiting for a moment that just won't come?" Sam Pulitzer speaks to us, the viewers, with a series of photographs that are at the center of this publication and were also at the core of the exhibition held at Kunsthaus Glarus in 2019. In addition to several generic, nonspecific landscapes and cityscapes, the images depict details of everyday things or places: a bouquet of flowers, a derelict shop, a sign, fresh-baked bread—observations of particular scenes and infrastructures, fetishized or almost comical objects the artist encounters as a resident of a city. These distanced, pedestrian, seductive, promising motifs serve as literal backdrops for the questions the artist poses. They are printed in subtitle style under the images on Plexiglass plates. For whom are they intended? Are they testing us, the audience? The artists and those interested in a particular attitude? Or are they a self-inquiry? If we think we have made out an addressee or a clear, critical position, the next questions—they mostly contain a contradiction—may well lead us off in a different direction again. The questions that accrue, which bring into play truisms regarding the relationship between the individual and society, between life and work, create a supposed intimacy. They are about potential individuality. What kind of life do we lead and what kind of life do you lead? How can we optimize it and in what ways do we want to improve it? *The Premise of a Better Life* is directed inward as well; not only to Sam Pulitzer, the individual, but perhaps to a nebulous "we." Under which material and political conditions are artists working today? What does artistic authorship mean in relation to the art market or a society in crisis for instance? The photographs portray New York almost without exception. The nondescript, rarely location-specific images do not document the city, but portray New York as a "sunken horizon," a pale reflection of a model city, a center of attraction and a place of longing. Unique and yet exemplary, ostensibly universally relevant. Sam Pulitzer, who is interested in literature and has developed his own writing practice over many years, uses his own texts in his works as well as quotes from literature, theory and pop culture. At first glance, his work with language and its legibility suggests accessibility. These montages, however, do not offer a clear narrative, but a complex, personal, at times satirical image of the present age and its promise. Some of the sources used are decoded; others are kept hidden or fictionalized and modified—reflecting how information is structured today. The intention of these gaps is not to exclude the viewer from meaning. Rather, they pose questions, such as who speaks for whom, or how the personal relates to the public, and thus implicitly how art and artists might adopt a political and social stance. The allegorical configurations of image and text depict hegemony and violence on a grand scale; on a macro level they dissect power relations and our infrequent inability to escape these conditions of "inside" and "outside."

«Kannst du dich dir leisten?» «Wartest du auf einen Moment, der einfach nicht kommen will?» Sam Pulitzer spricht uns, die Betrachter:innen, mit seiner Serie von Fotografien an, die ebenfalls Ende 2019 im Zentrum der Ausstellung im Kunsthaus Glarus standen. Nebst einigen generischen, unspezifischen Landschaften und Stadtansichten zeigen die Bilder Details alltäglicher Dinge oder Orte: einen Blumenstrauss, ein heruntergekommenes Ladenlokal, ein Hinweisschild, frisch gebackenes Brot. Es sind Beobachtungen von Kulissen und Infrastrukturen, fetischisierte oder skurrile Objekte, denen der Künstler als Bewohner dieser Stadt begegnet. Diese distanziert-langweiligen und doch verführerisch-versprechenden Motive dienen wortwörtlich als Bildgrund für die Fragen, die Sam Pulitzer stellt. Im Stil eines Untertitels werden sie, aufgedruckt auf Plexiglasscheiben, über die Bilder gelegt. An wen richten sie sich? Wollen sie uns, das Publikum, die Künstler:innen und Interessierten, auf eine Haltung prüfen, oder sind sie eine Selbstbefragung? Wenn wir glauben, eine:n Adressat:in oder eine kritische Position ausgemacht zu haben, so führt uns die nächste Frage - die meisten beinhalten übrigens einen Widerspruch - womöglich gleich wieder in eine andere Richtung. Die aneinandergereihten Fragen bringen Gemeinplätze der Beziehung zwischen Individuum und Gesellschaft, zwischen Leben und Arbeit ins Spiel und schaffen vermeintliche Intimität. Sie handeln von möglicher Individualität. Was führen wir und was führt ihr für ein Leben? Wie können wir es optimieren, und in welche Richtung wollen wir es verbessern?

The Premise of a Better Life richtet sich auch nach innen; nicht nur auf den Künstler als Person, sondern auch auf ein unscharfes «Wir». Unter welchen materiellen und politischen Bedingungen arbeiten Künstler:innen heute? Was bedeutet künstlerische Autor:innenschaft etwa in Bezug zum Kunstmarkt oder einer Gesellschaft in der Krise? Die Fotografien porträtieren fast ausnahmslos New York. Die gesichtslosen, nur ganz selten lokalisierbaren Bilder dokumentieren die Stadt nicht, sondern zeigen New York als «gesunkenen Horizont», Abglanz einer Modellstadt, Anziehungspunkt und Sehnsuchtsort. Einzigartig und doch vorbildhaft, von vermeintlich universaler Gültigkeit. Sam Pulitzer verwendet in seinen Werken eigene Texte und Zitate aus Literatur, Theorie und Popkultur. Obwohl die Arbeit mit Sprache auf den ersten Blick Zugänglichkeit respektive Lesbarkeit suggeriert, ergeben diese Montagen keine eindeutige Erzählung, aber ein komplexes, persönliches, stellenweise satirisches Bild der Jetzt-Zeit und ihren Versprechen. Manche der verwendeten Quellen werden entschlüsselt, andere verborgen gehalten oder fiktionalisiert und modifiziert. Sie spiegeln damit nicht zuletzt die Art und Weise wider, wie Information heute strukturiert ist. Diese Lücken zielen nicht darauf ab, die Betrachter:innen von Bedeutung auszuschliessen. Vielmehr stellen sie Fragen, etwa danach, wer für wen spricht oder wie das Persönliche mit dem Öffentlichen zusammenhängt, und damit implizit danach, wie Kunst und Künstler:innen eine politische und gesellschaftliche Haltung einnehmen könnten. Die allegorischen Bild-Text-Anordnungen zeigen im Grossen Hegemonien und Gewalt auf, im Kleinen sezieren sie Machtverhältnisse und unser nicht seltenes Unvermögen, uns diesen Bedingungen von «Innen» und «Aussen» zu entziehen.

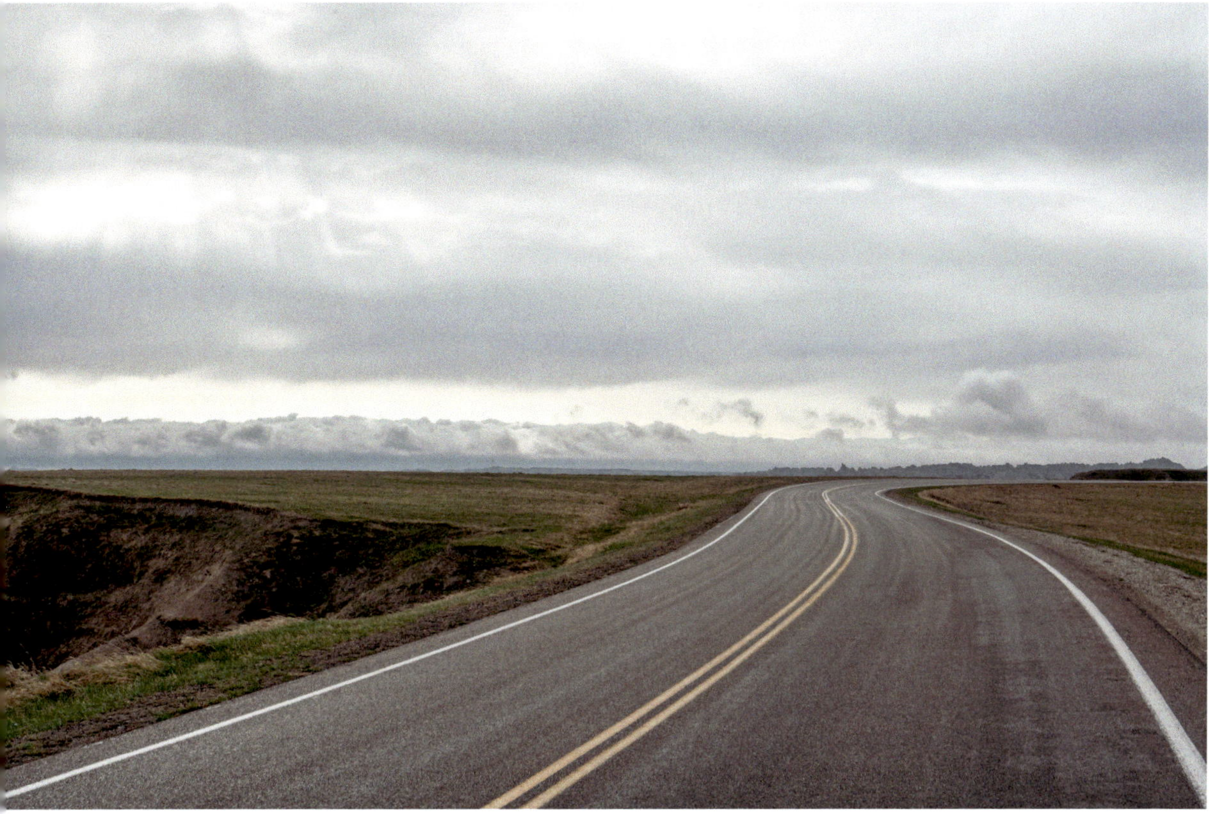

Can you afford yourself?

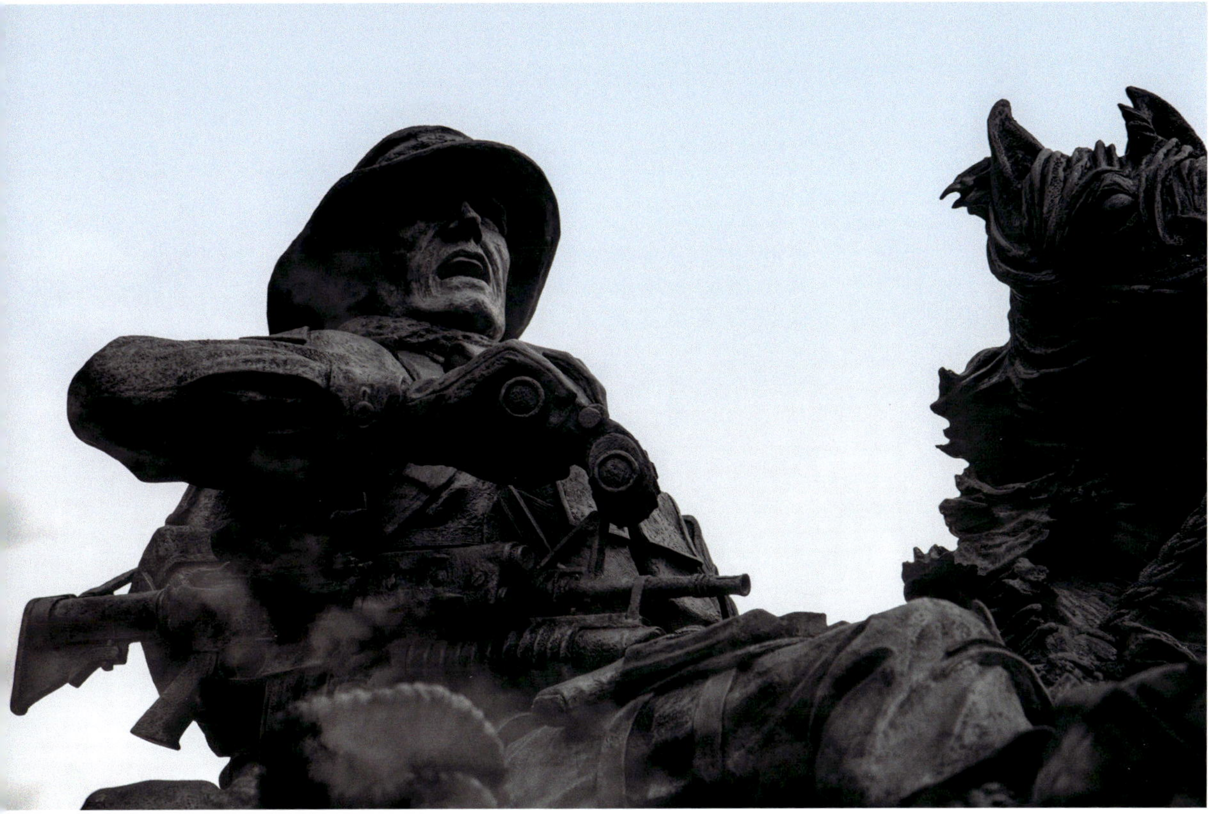

Can you see yourself as others do?

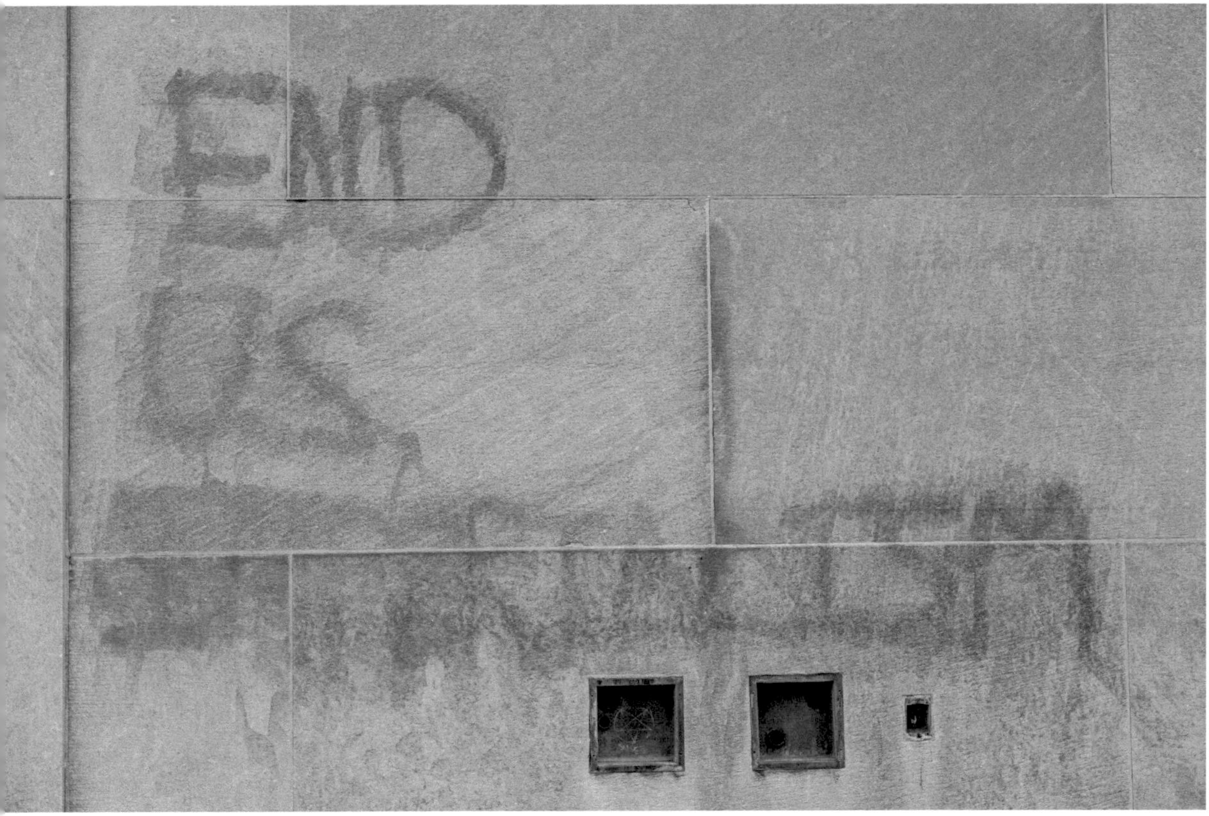

Can you fuck up and still get paid?

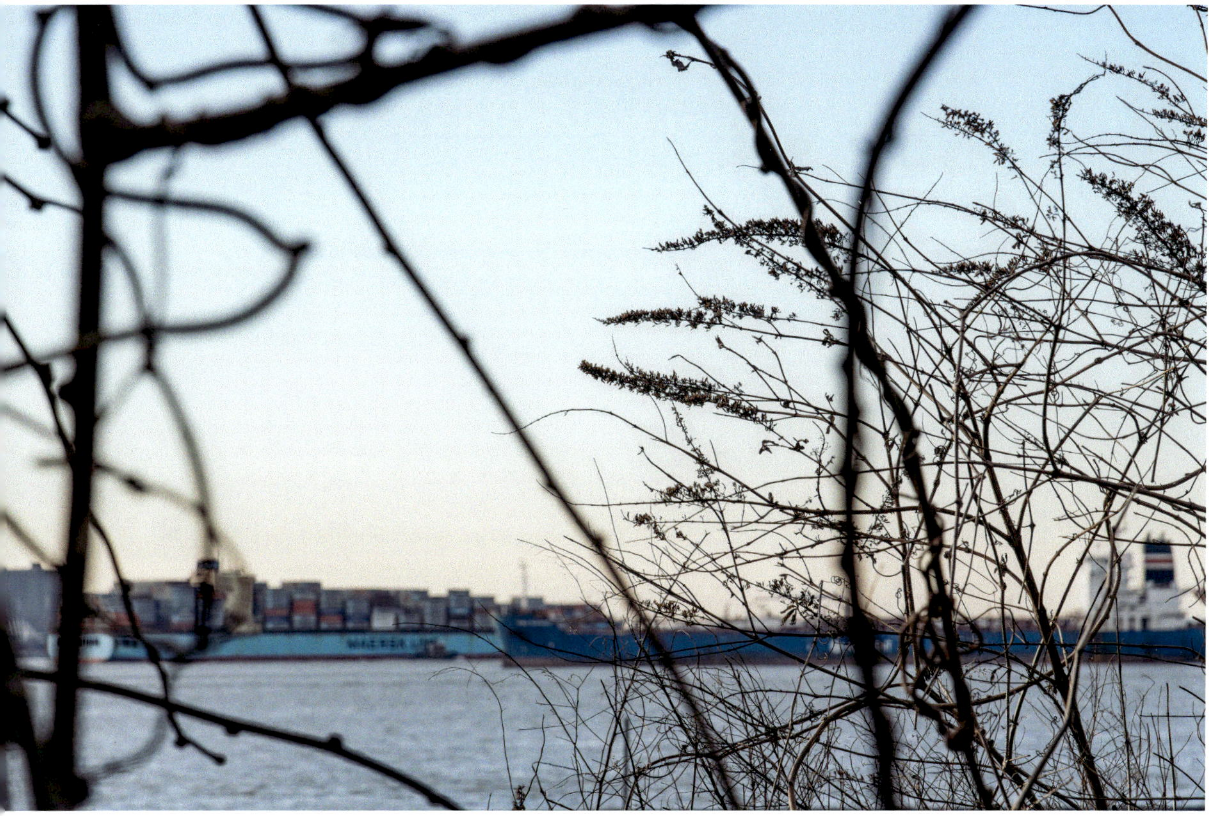

Is it a compromise to see life without compromise?

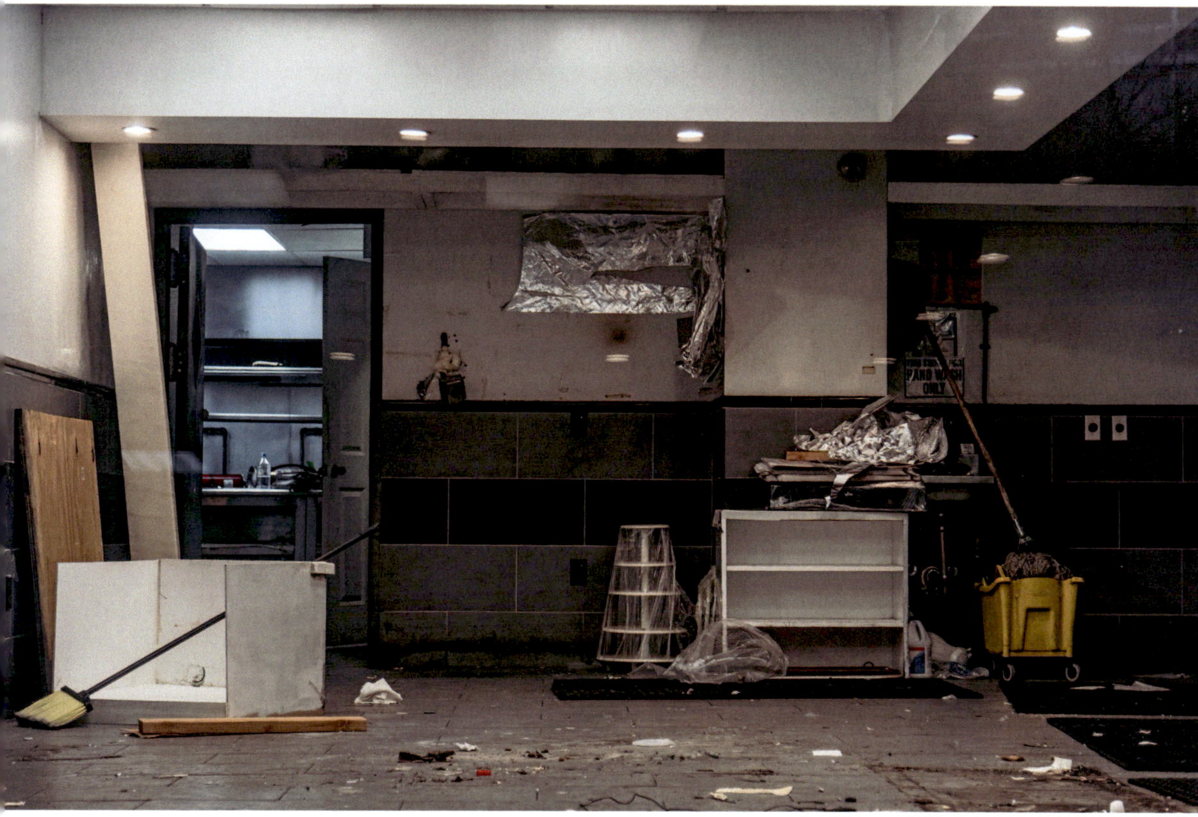

Should knowing better know better?

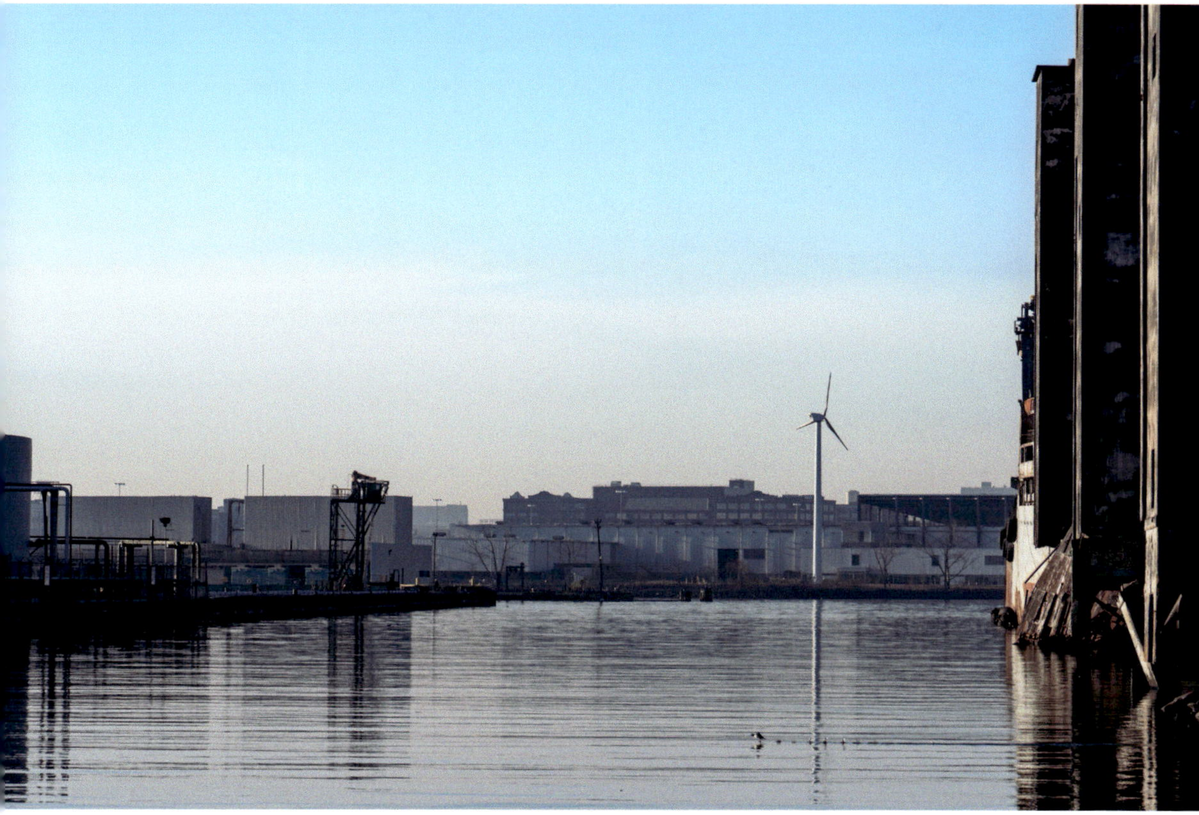

If you could change the world, what could make you too good to do so?

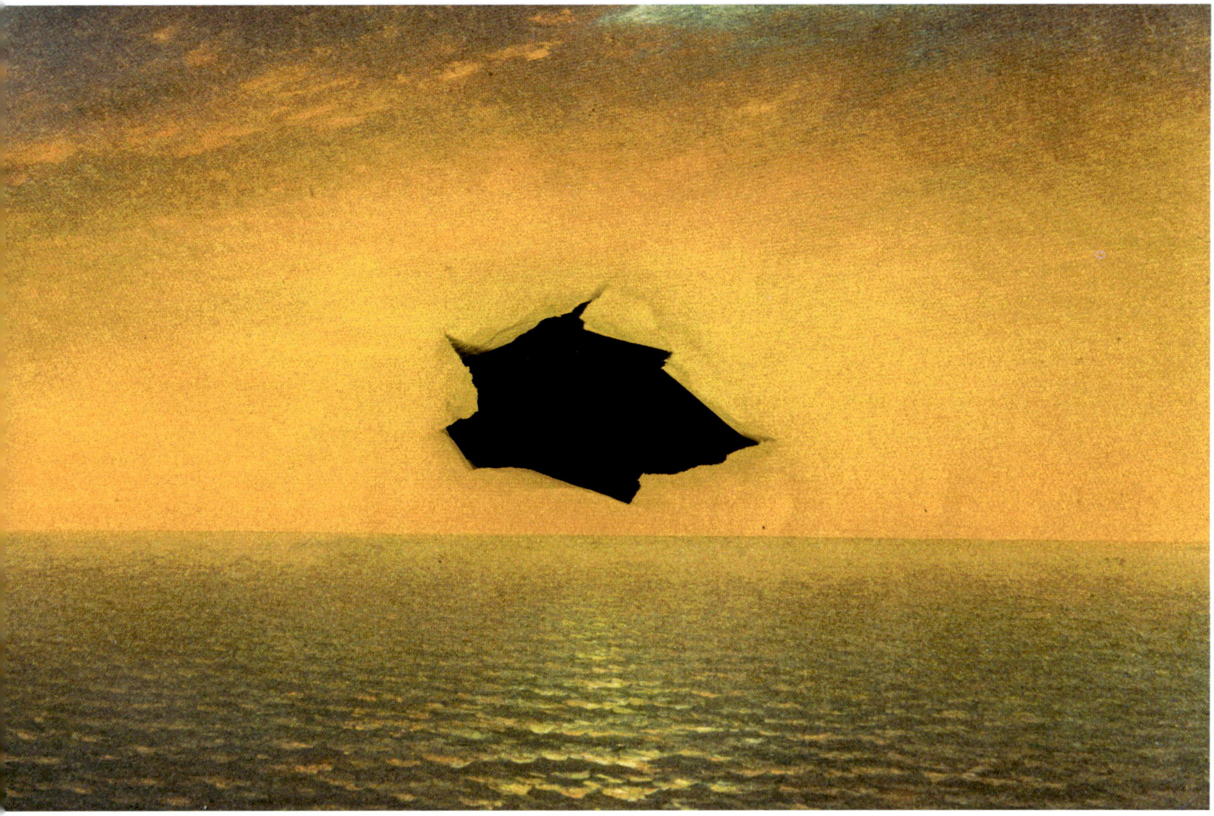

Have you known better but never bothered to protest?

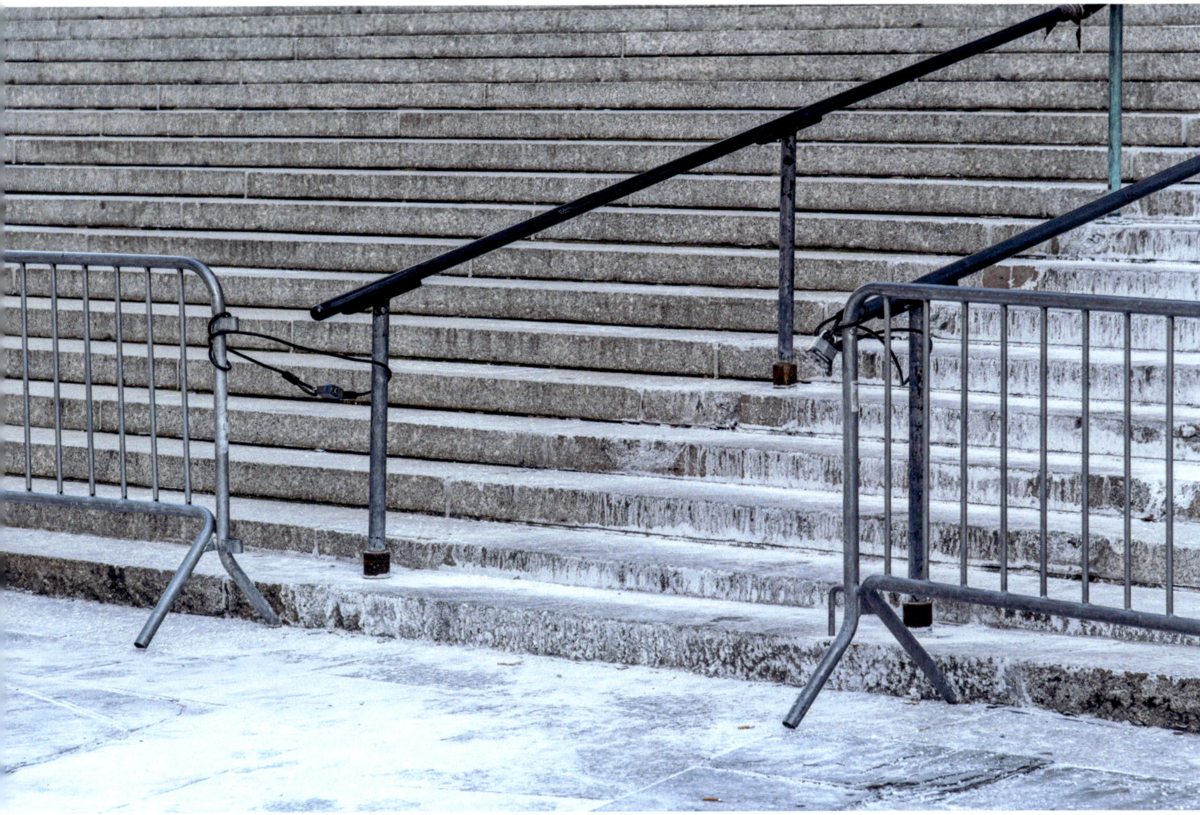

Are you guaranteed the recognition you require?

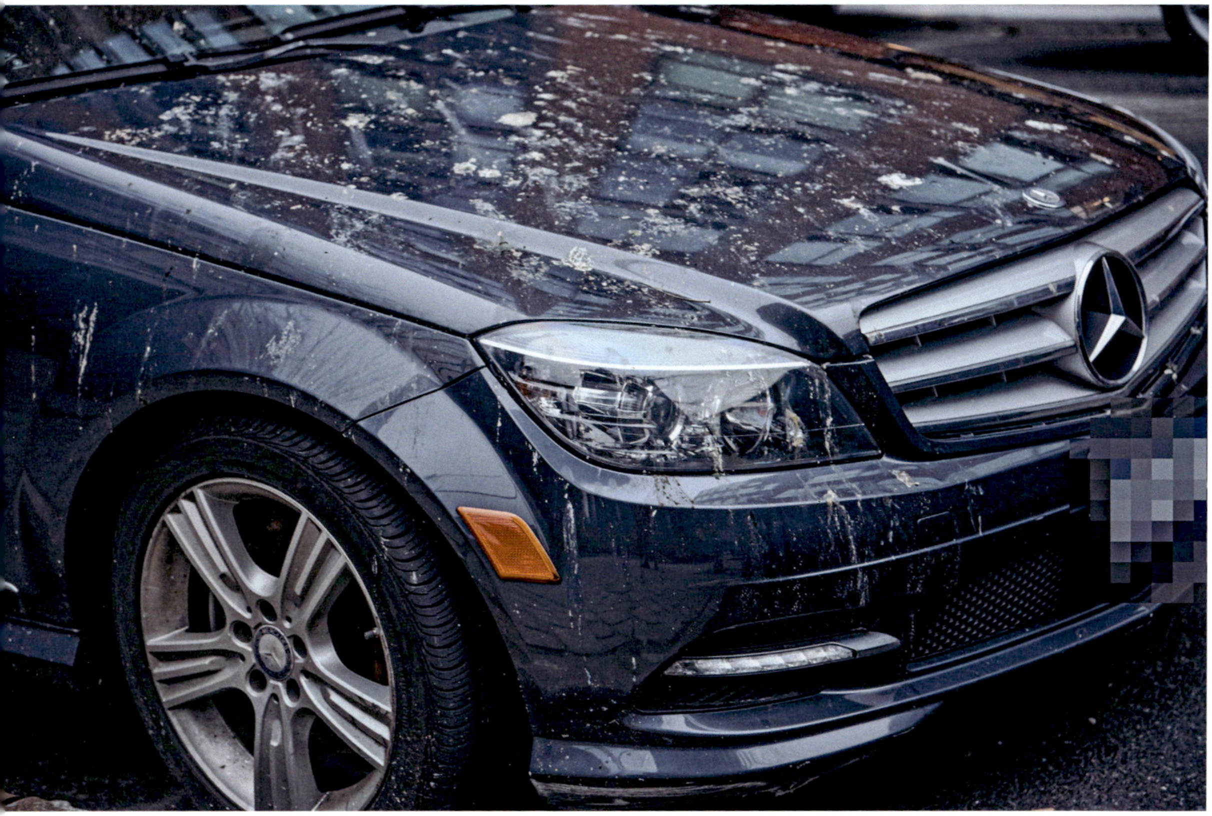

Why save when the value of your assets does it for you?

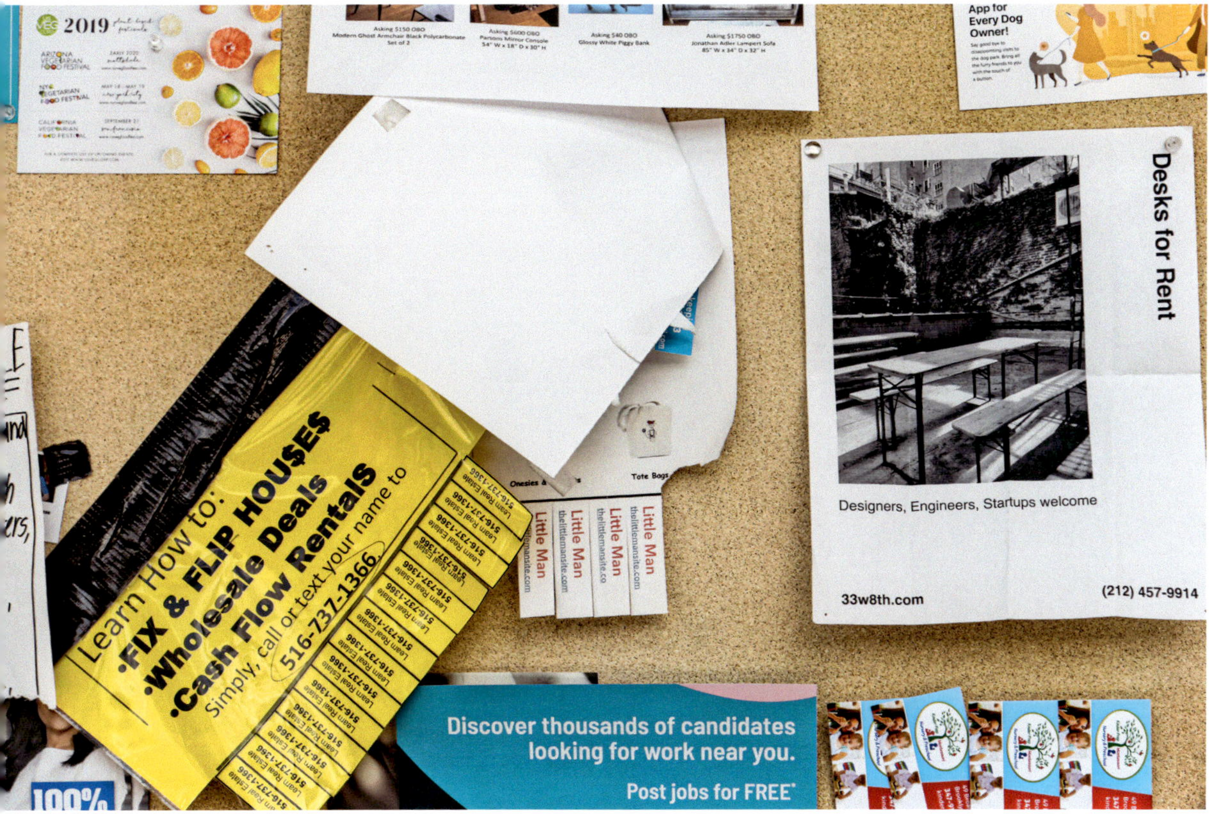

Can you explain how you earn a living to a child?

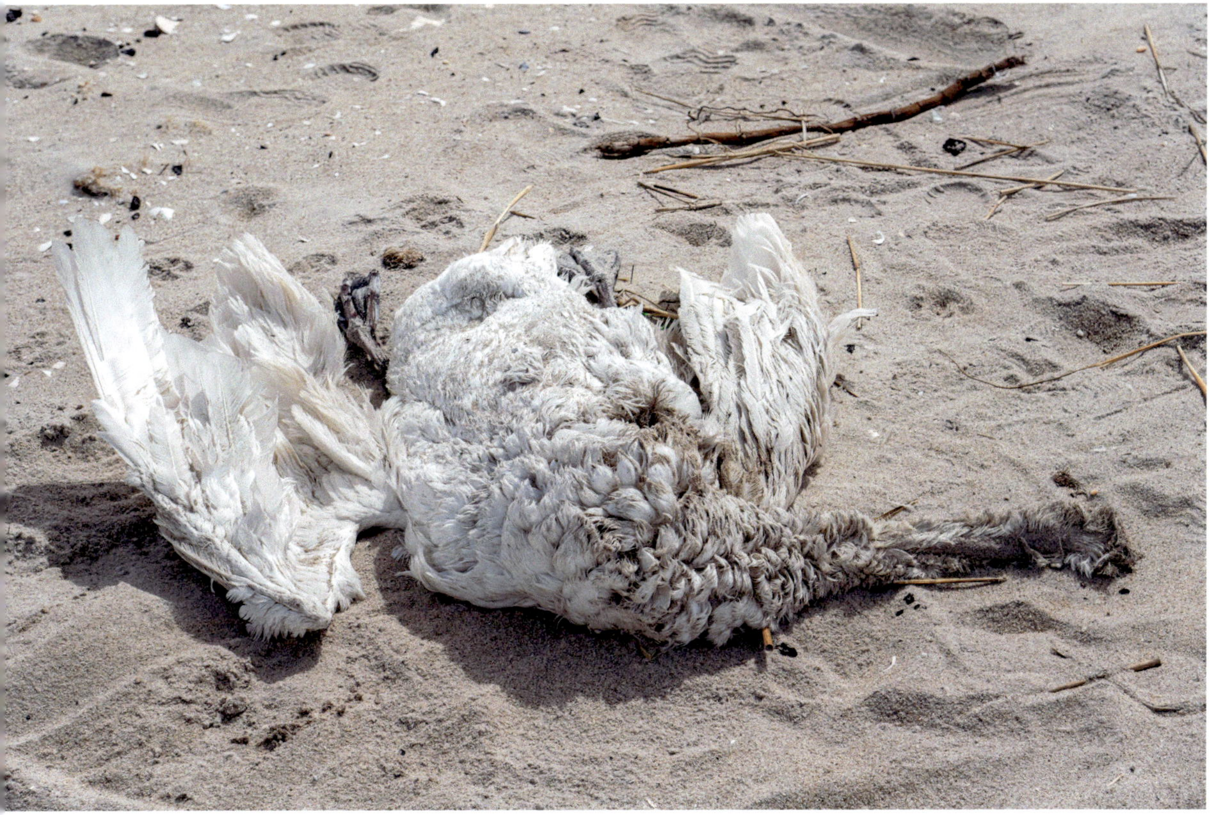

Are you waiting for a moment that just won’t come?

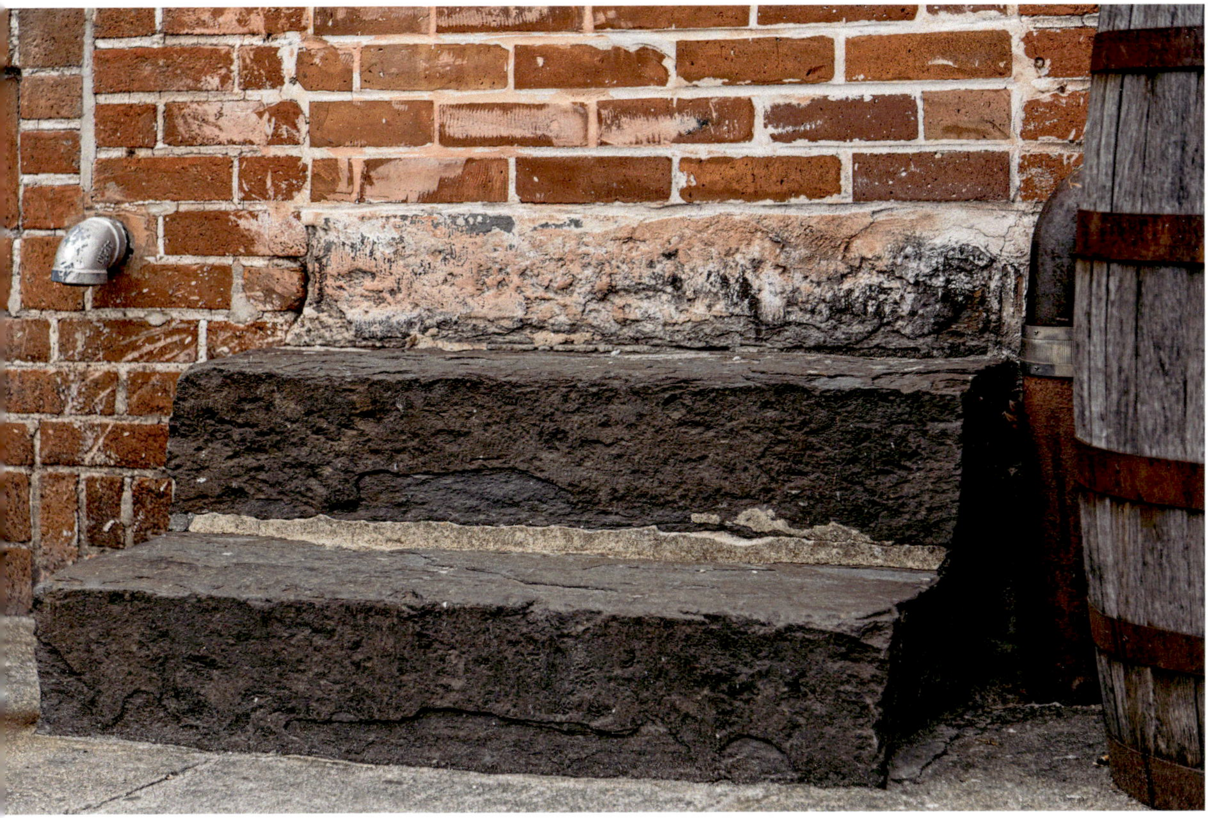

Are you waiting for a moment that's already arrived?

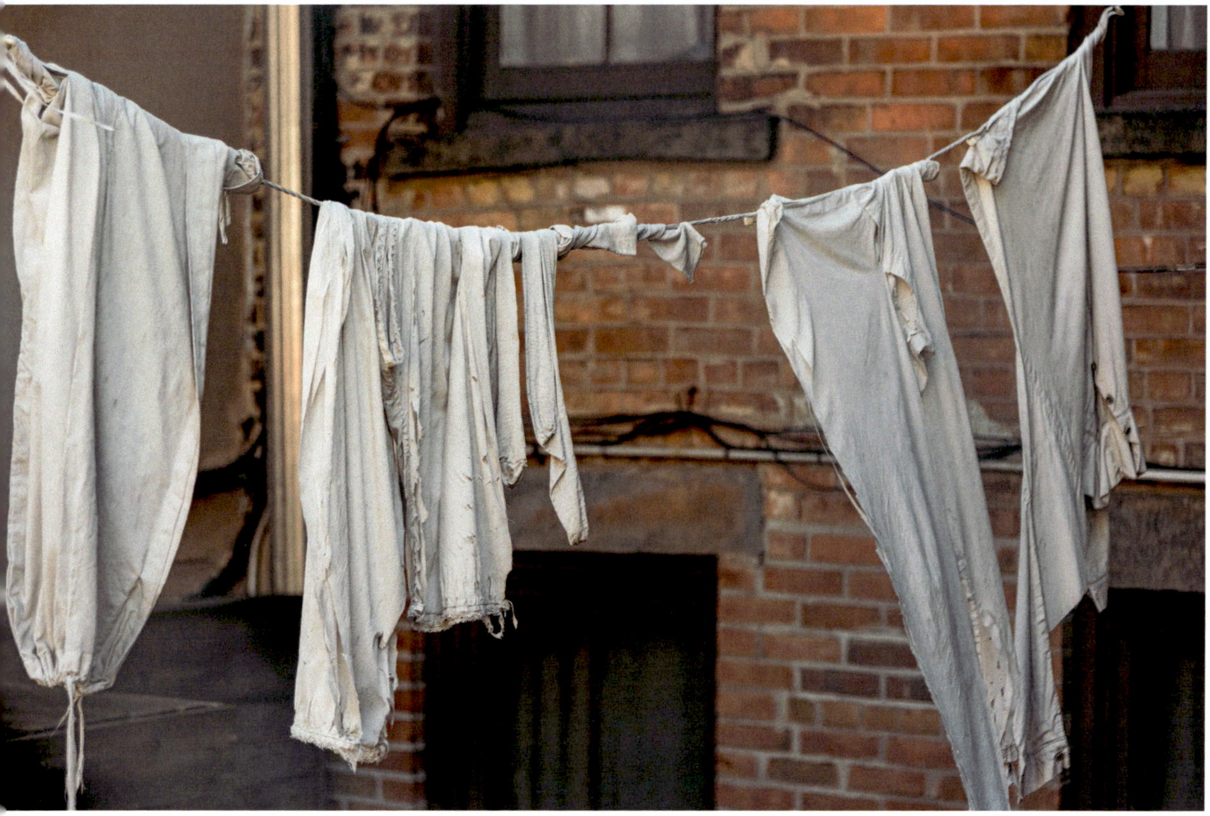

Are you able to profit by eliminating the conditions of its capture?

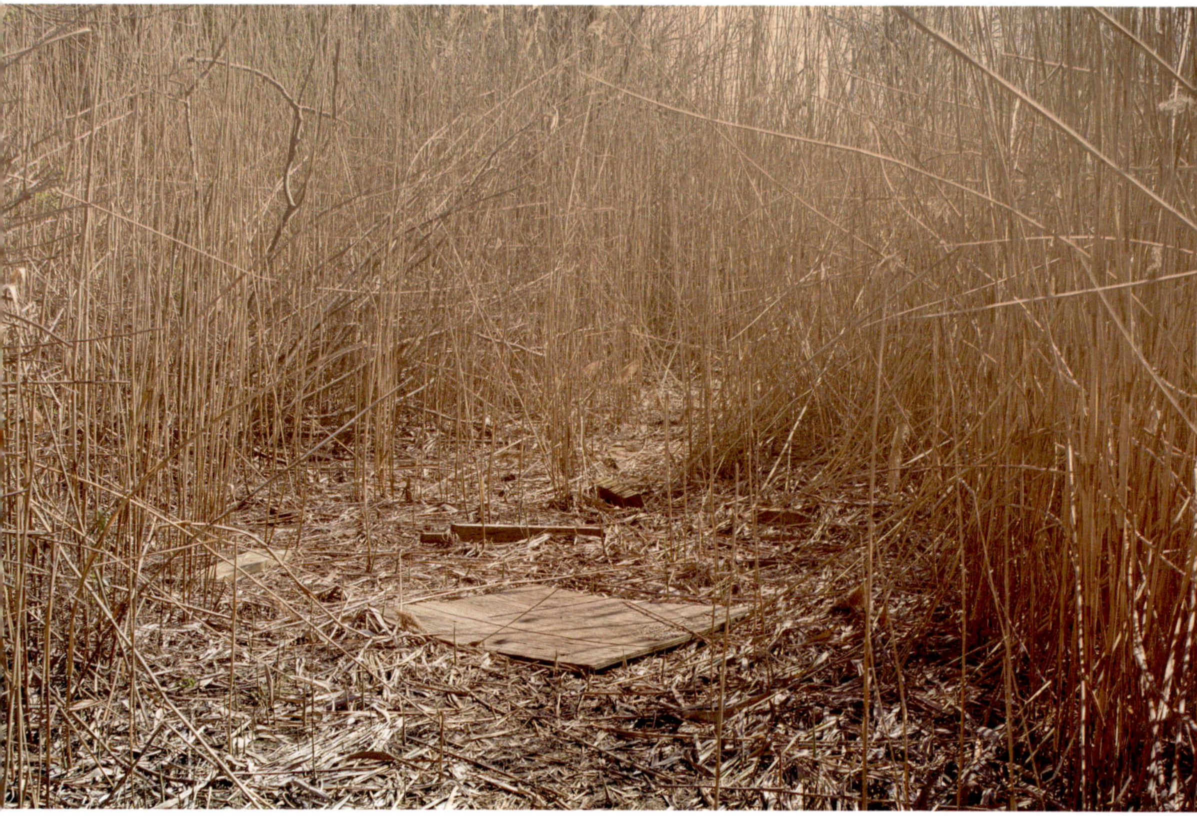

Have you chosen to live apart from the life into which you were born?

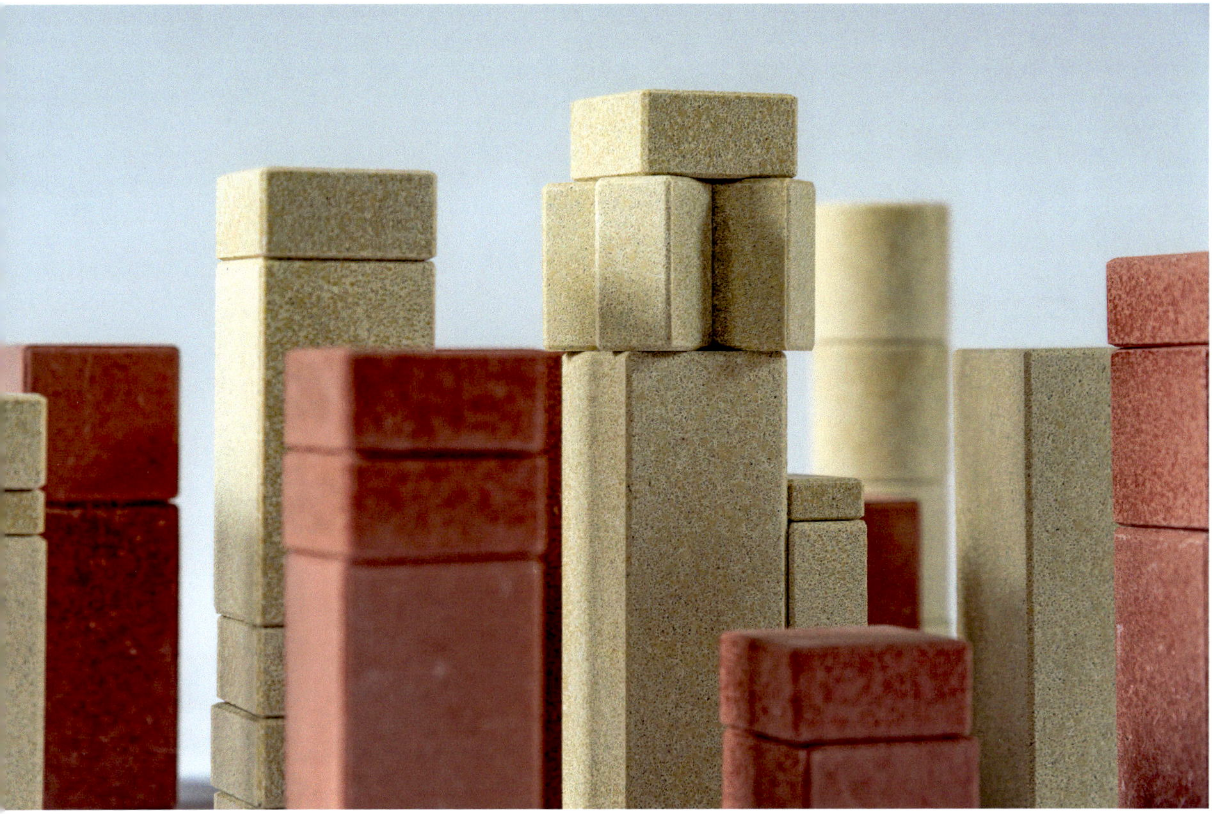

Will you always encounter the distance from where you started?

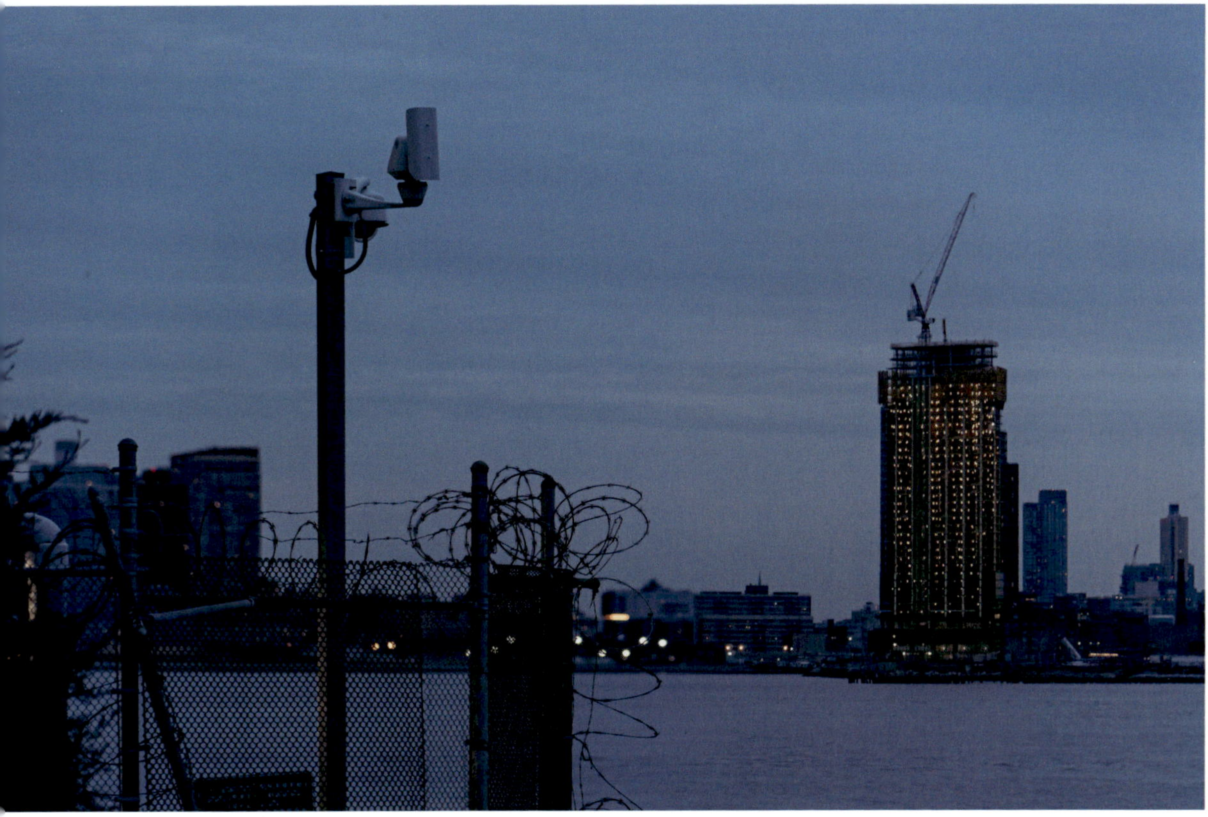

Do you see yourself as the person for whom you'll be remembered?

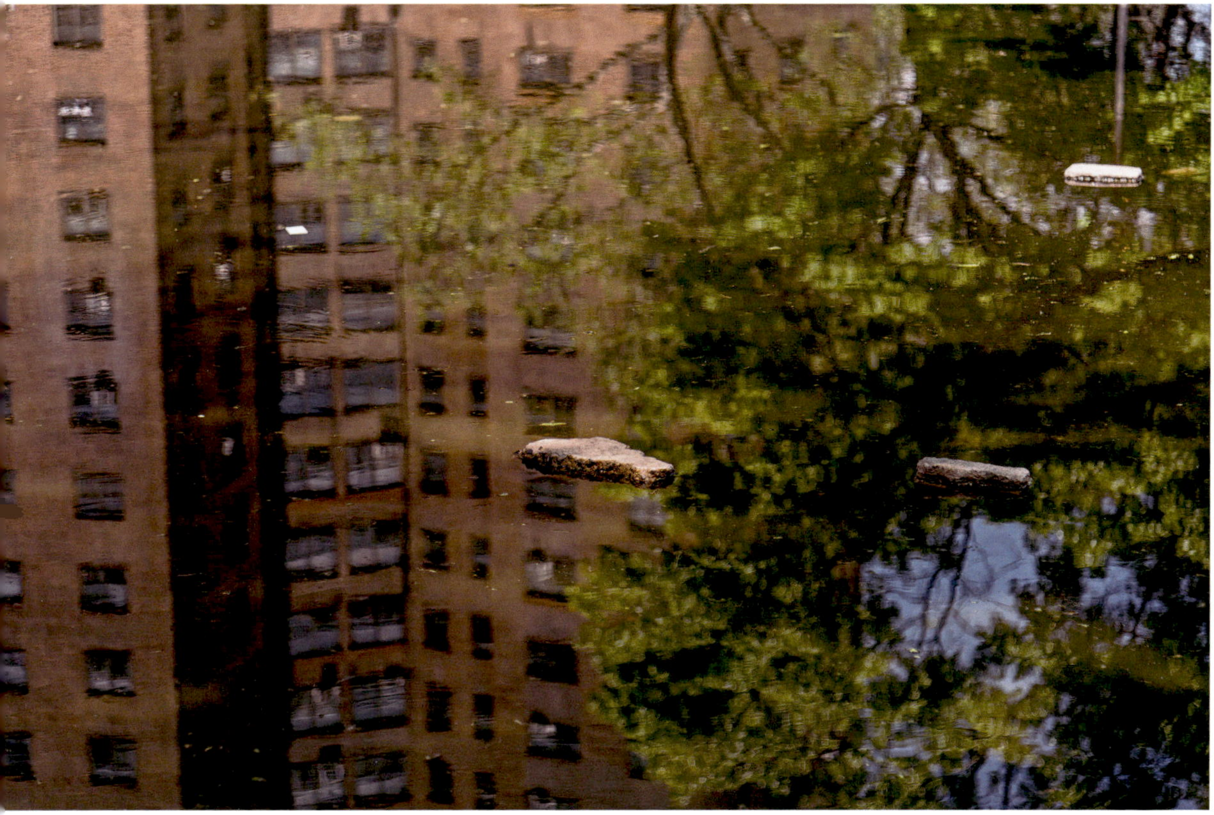

If there's not enough of everything, is nothing enough?

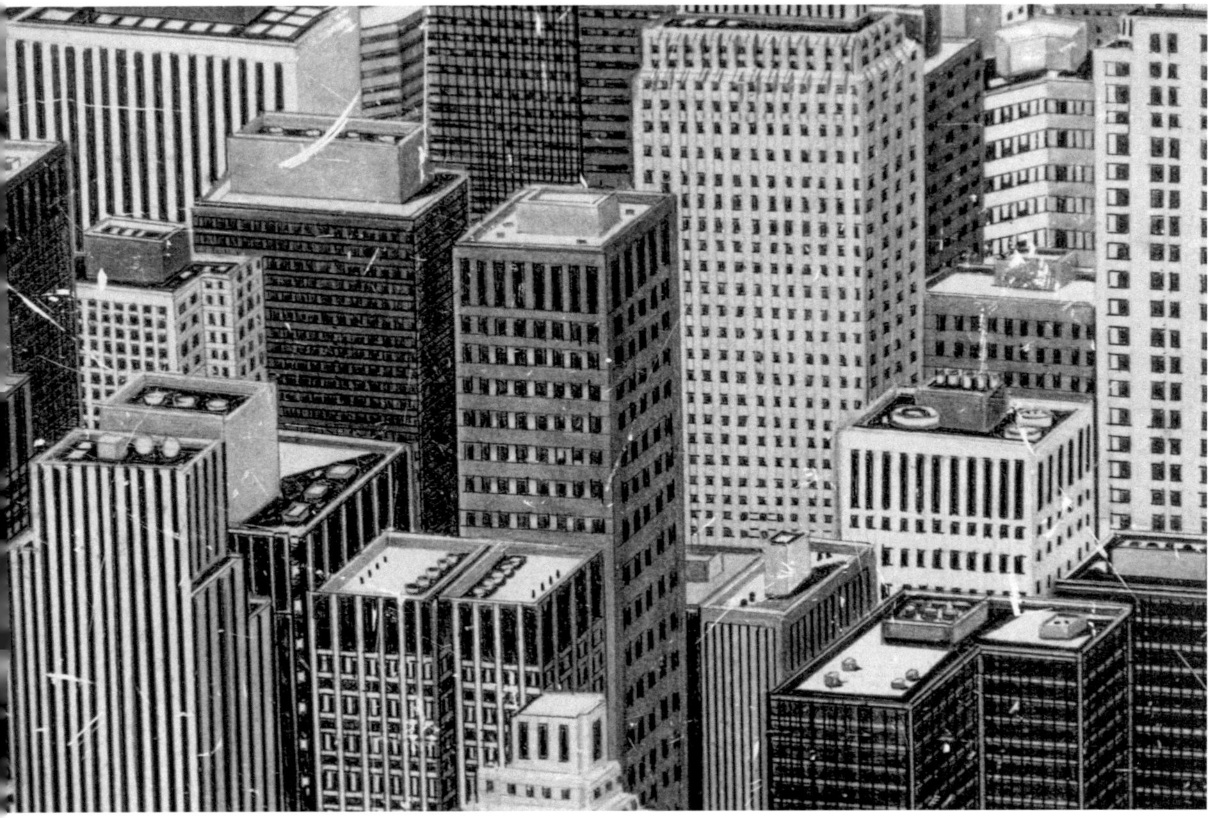

Can you bury your head so deeply in the ground that it'll sprout from the other side?

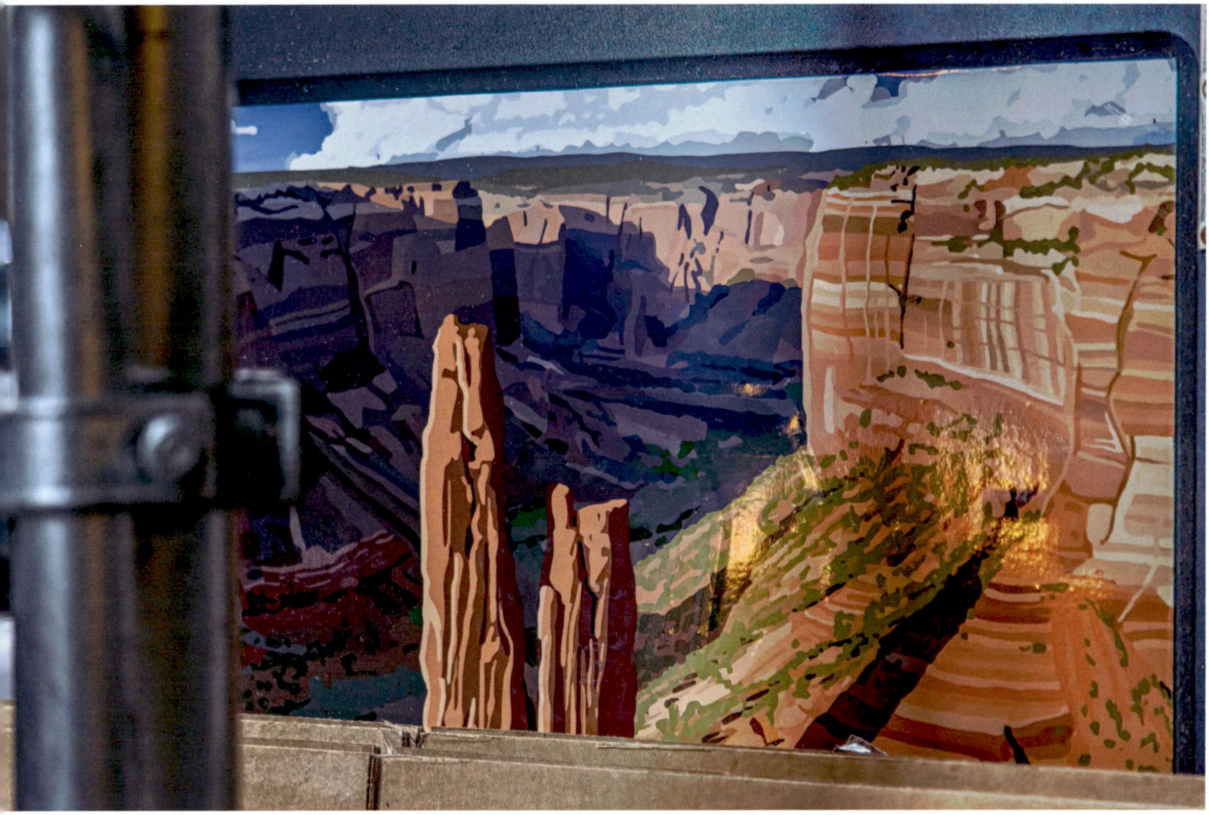

Is it a catastrophe if it is ordinary?

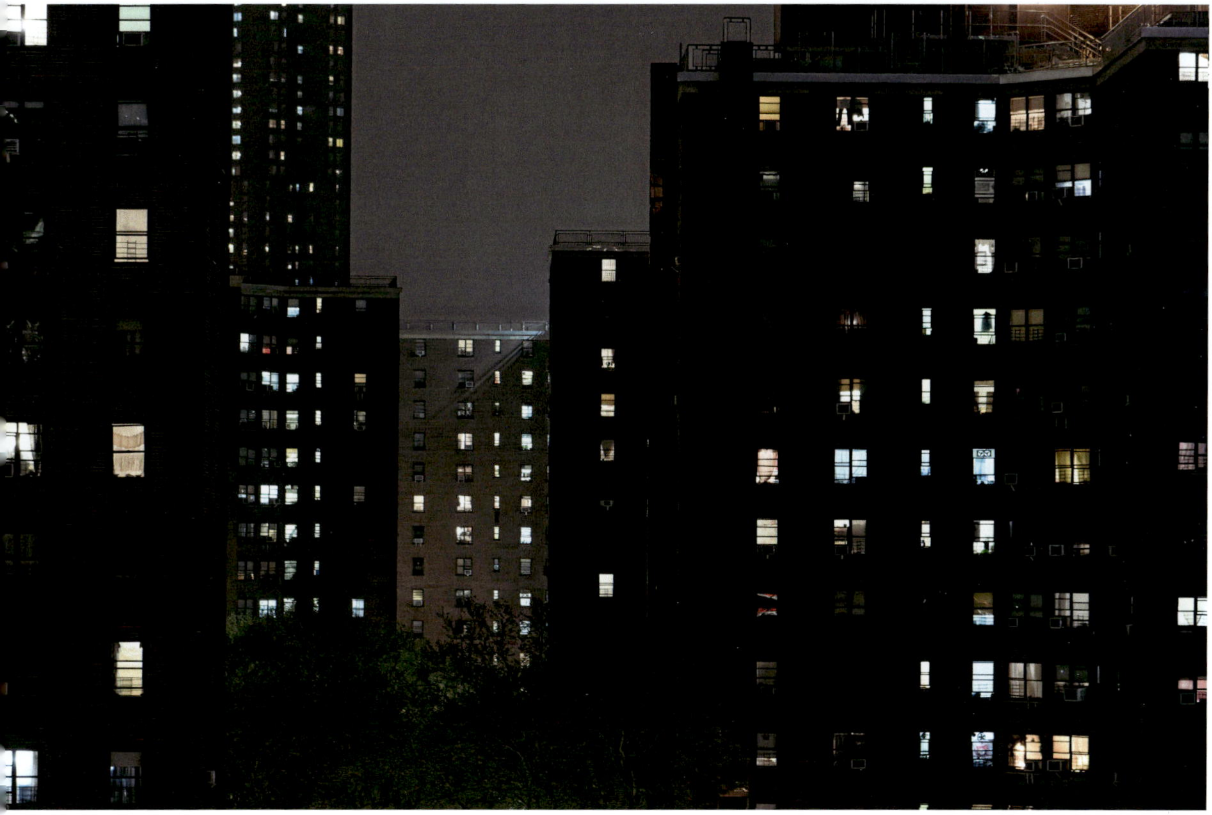

Does your desire count?

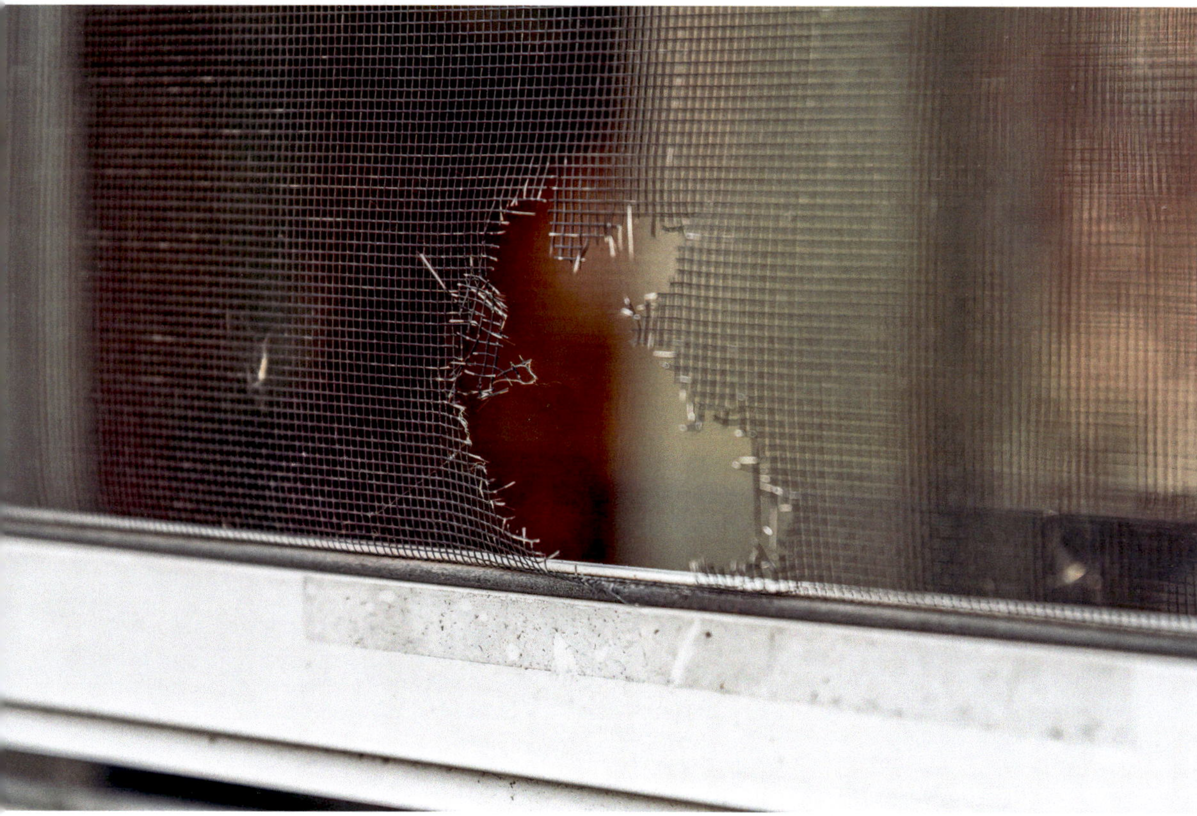

Are you stuck with what you don't have?

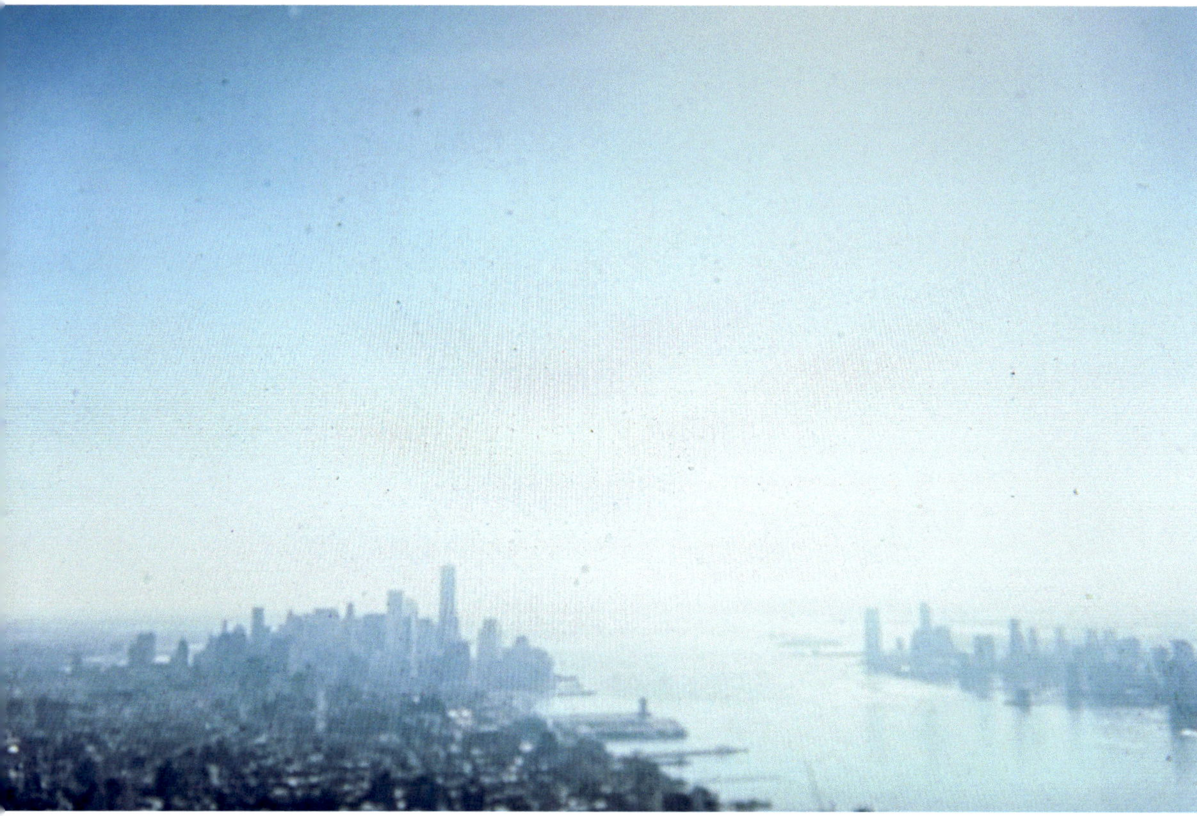

Are your senses tied to a form that produces pain elsewhere?

Four Ways to Spend Money

Whose money is spent		On whom money is spent: Yourself	On whom money is spent: Someone else
	Yours	Economize and seek highest value	Economize, but don't seek highest value
	Someone else's	Don't economize but seek highest value	Don't economize and don't seek highest value

Source: Council of Economic Advisors

Do you live up to your own expectations?

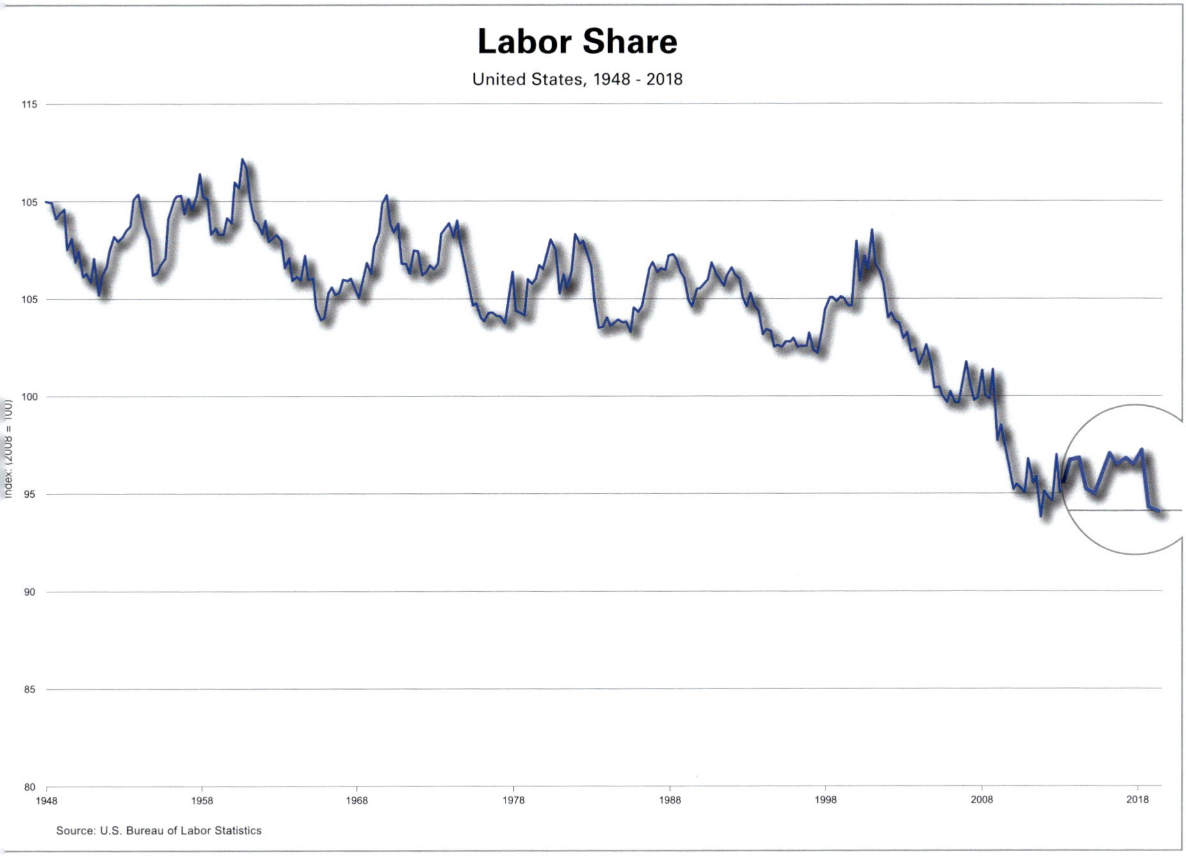

Have you lost the words that once came effortlessly?

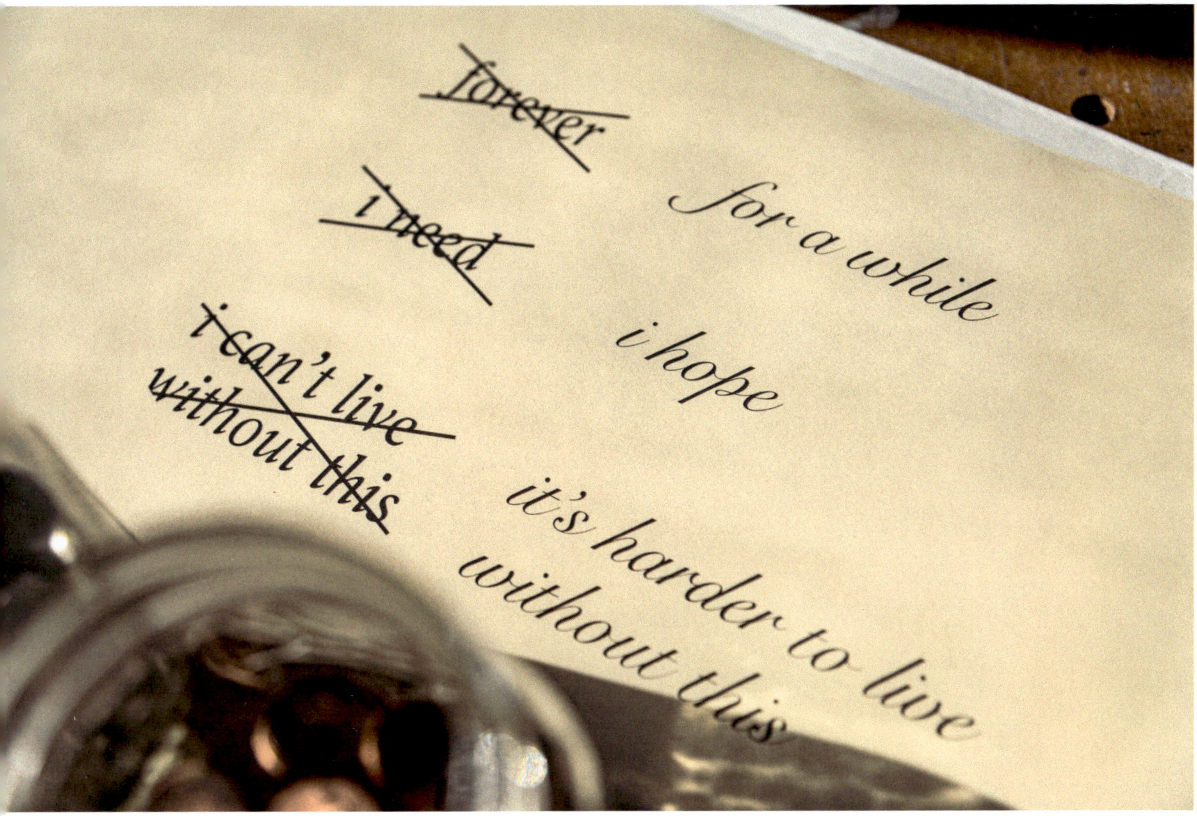

Are you willing to ask for as much as you are willing to give?

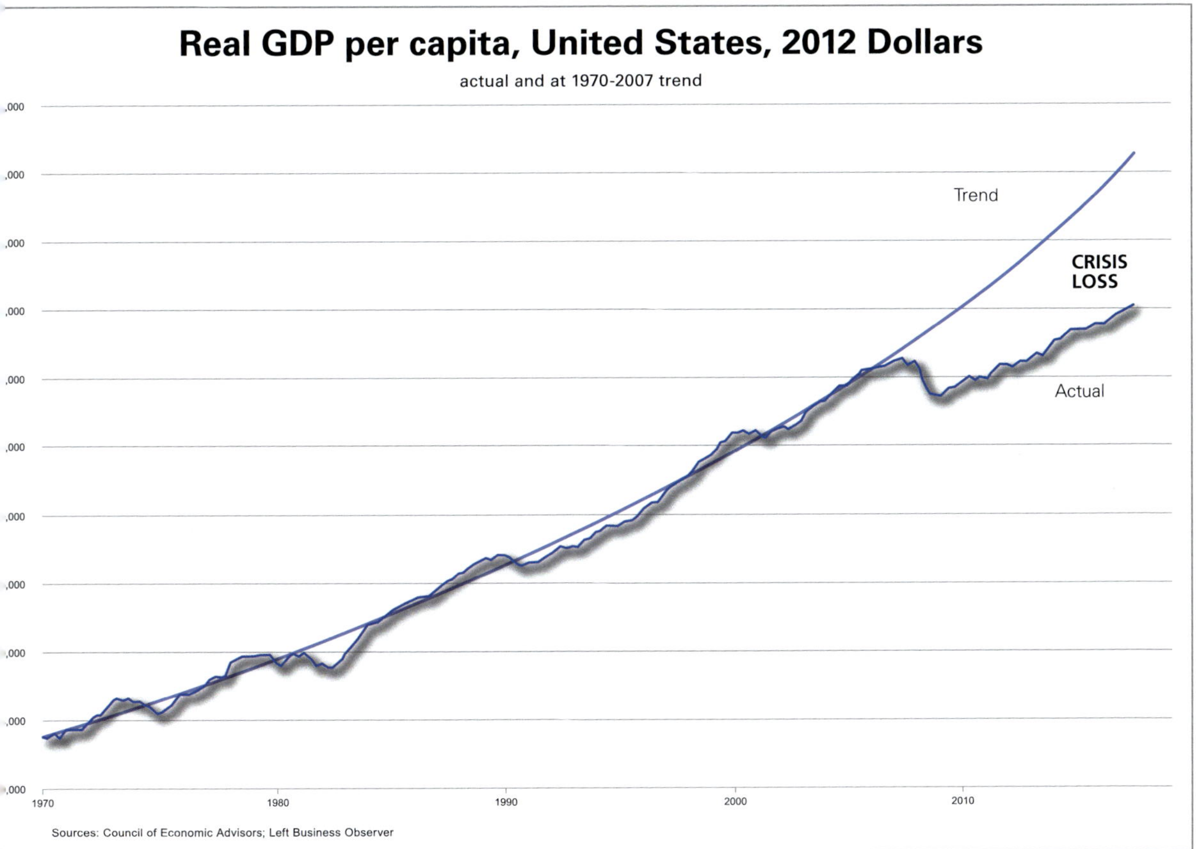

Do you trust happiness?

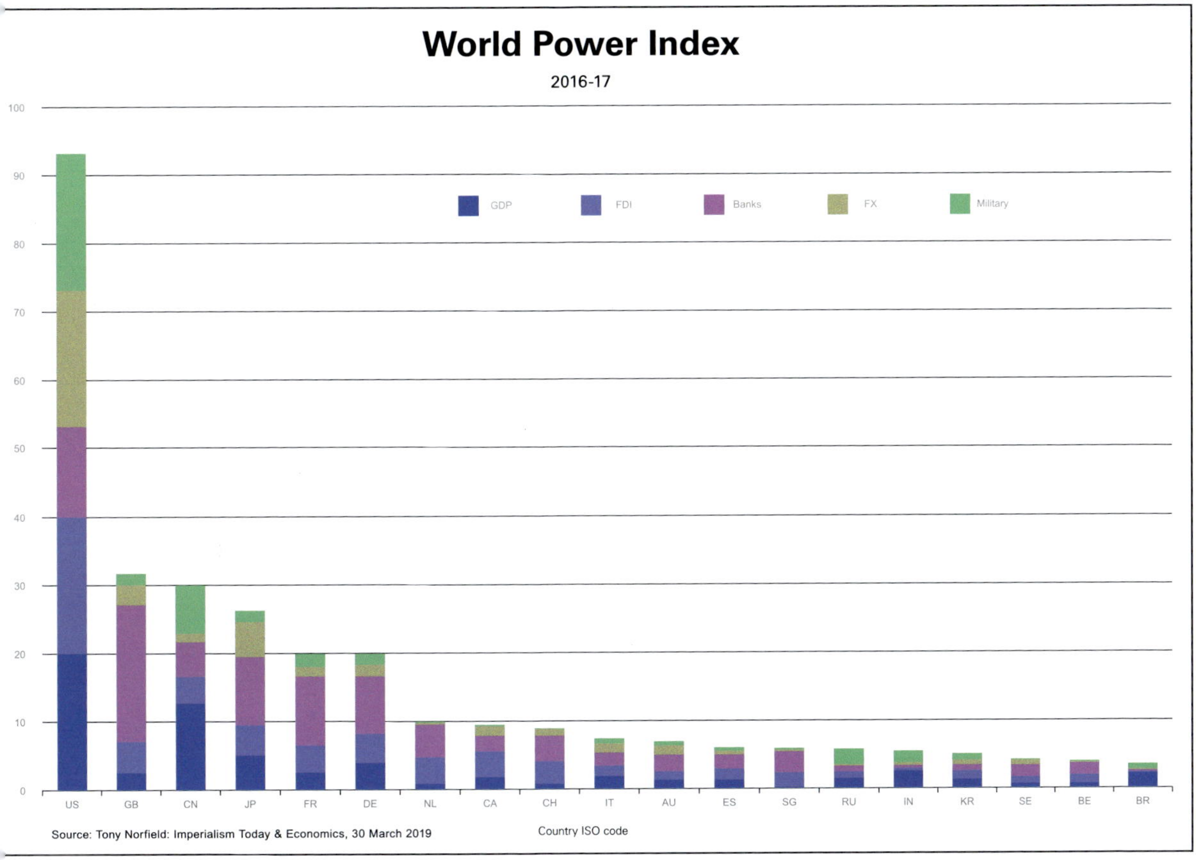

Is your exercise of rational self-interest someone else's problem?

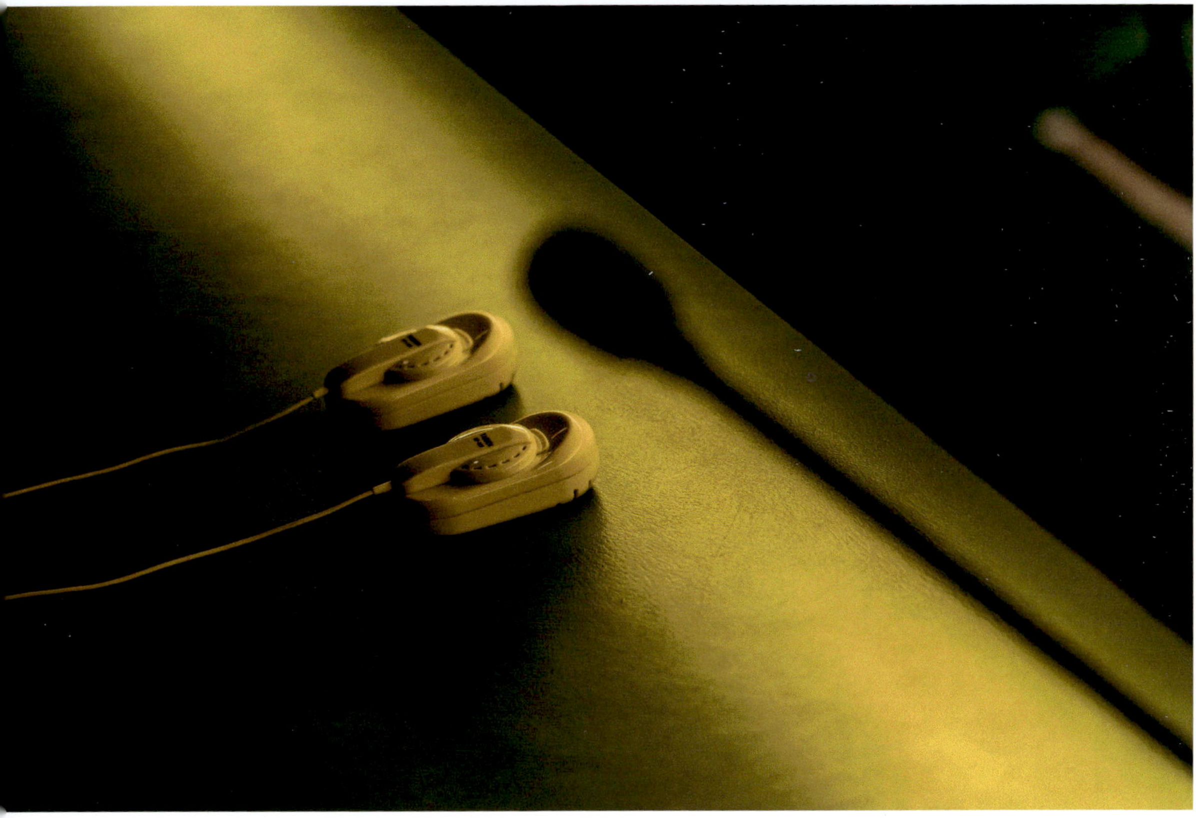

Are you in a position to talk about what you want?

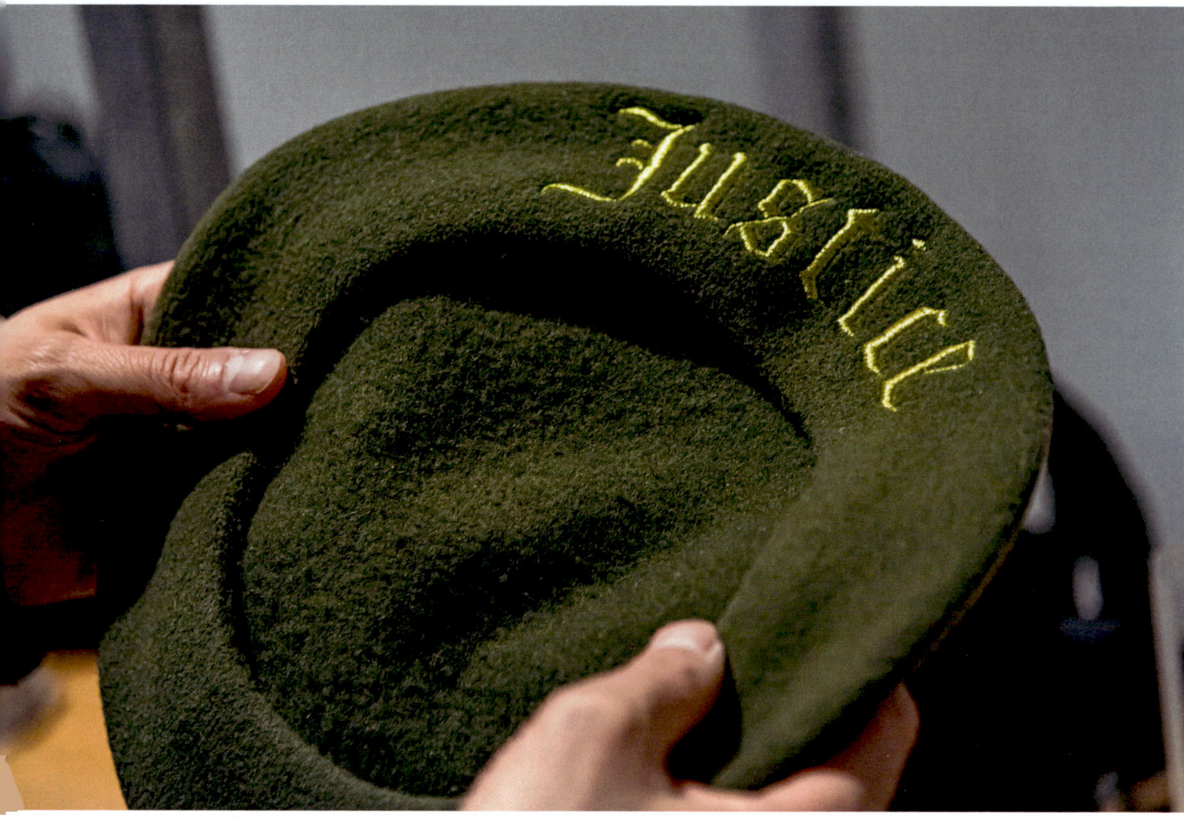

Is the correct line enough?

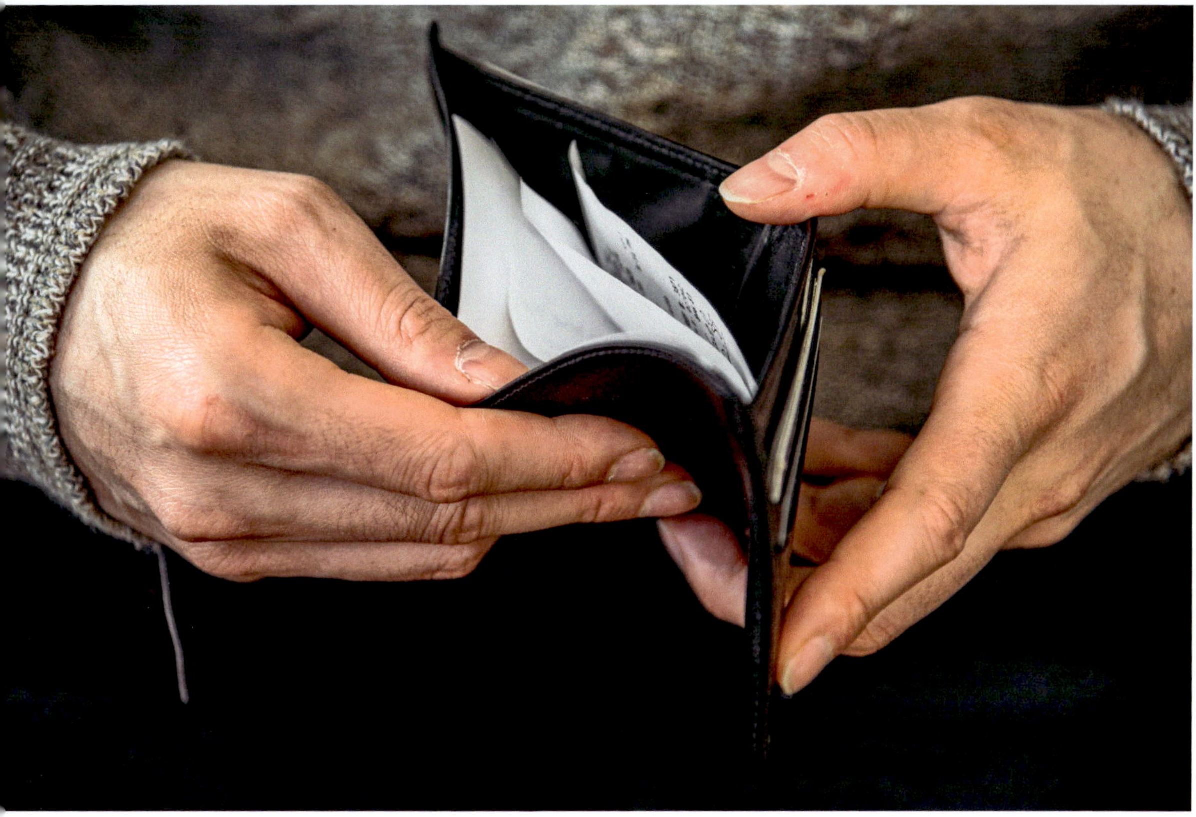

Is there a subsitute for participation?

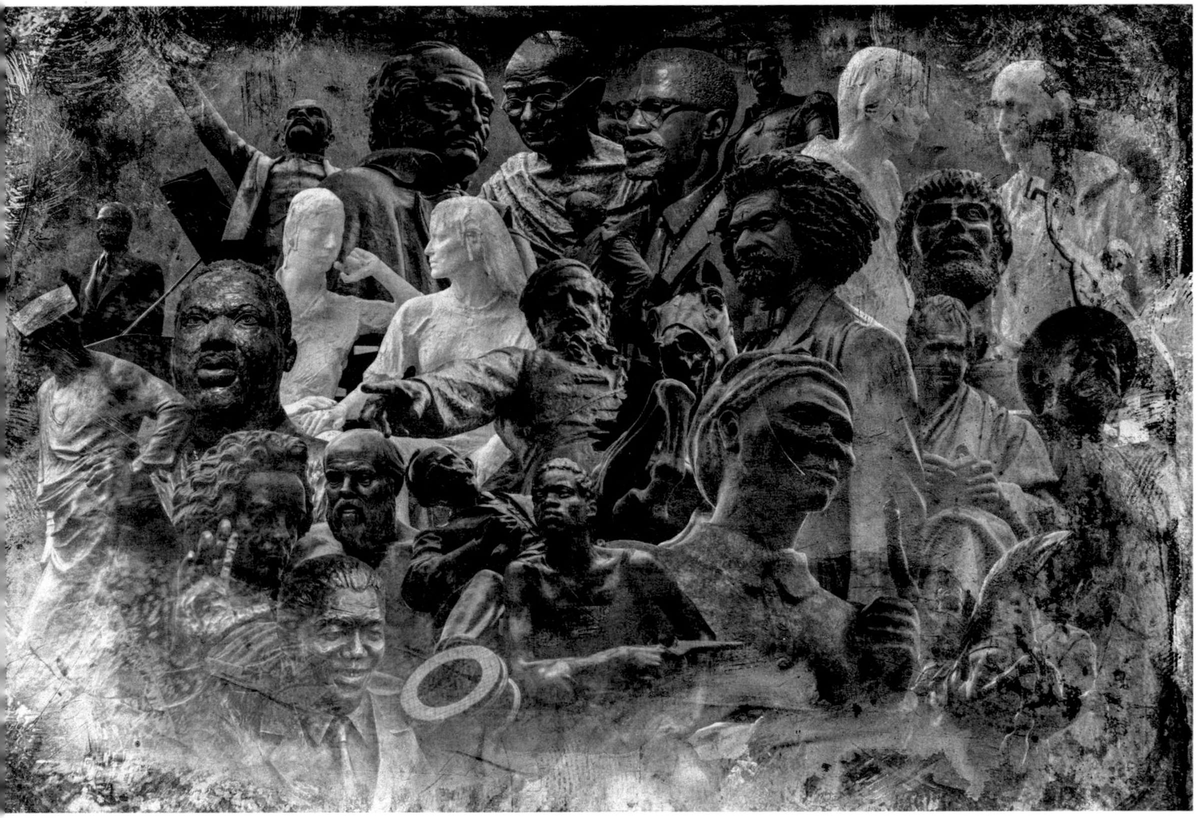

Are some things worth repeating?

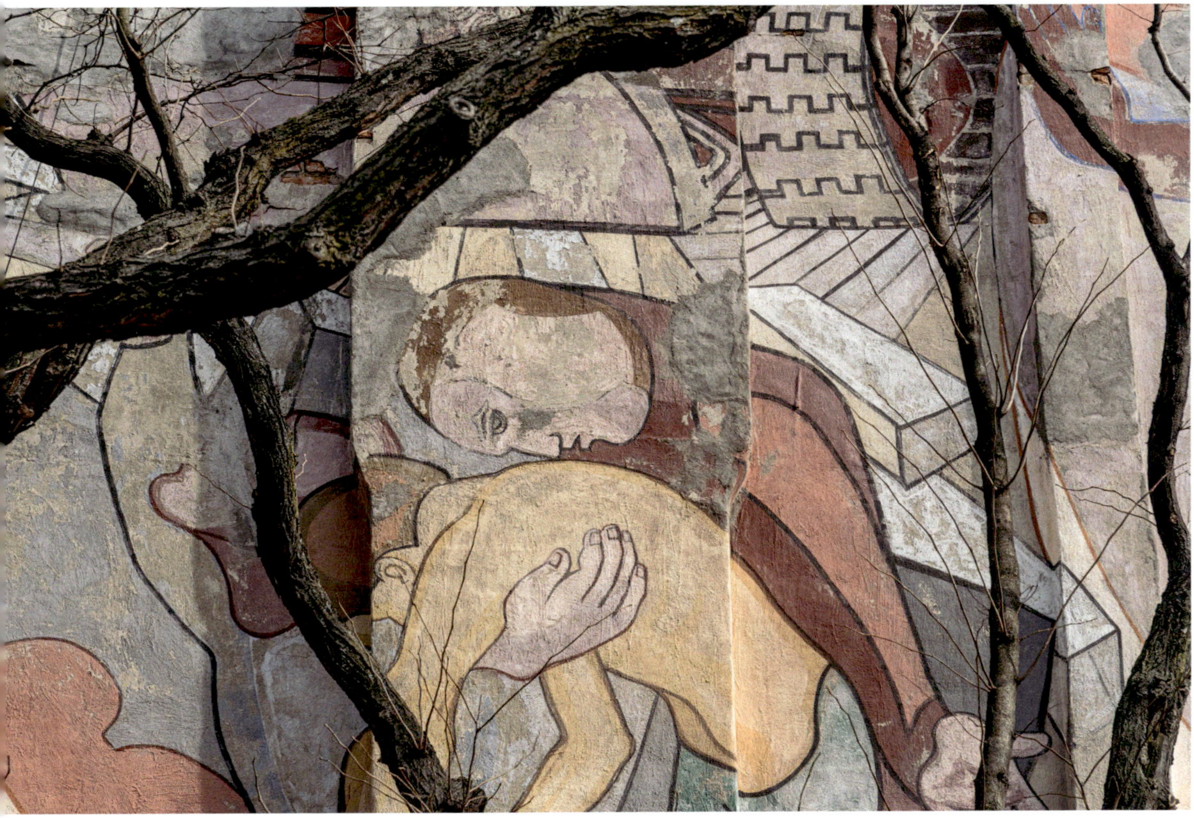

Is defeat failure?

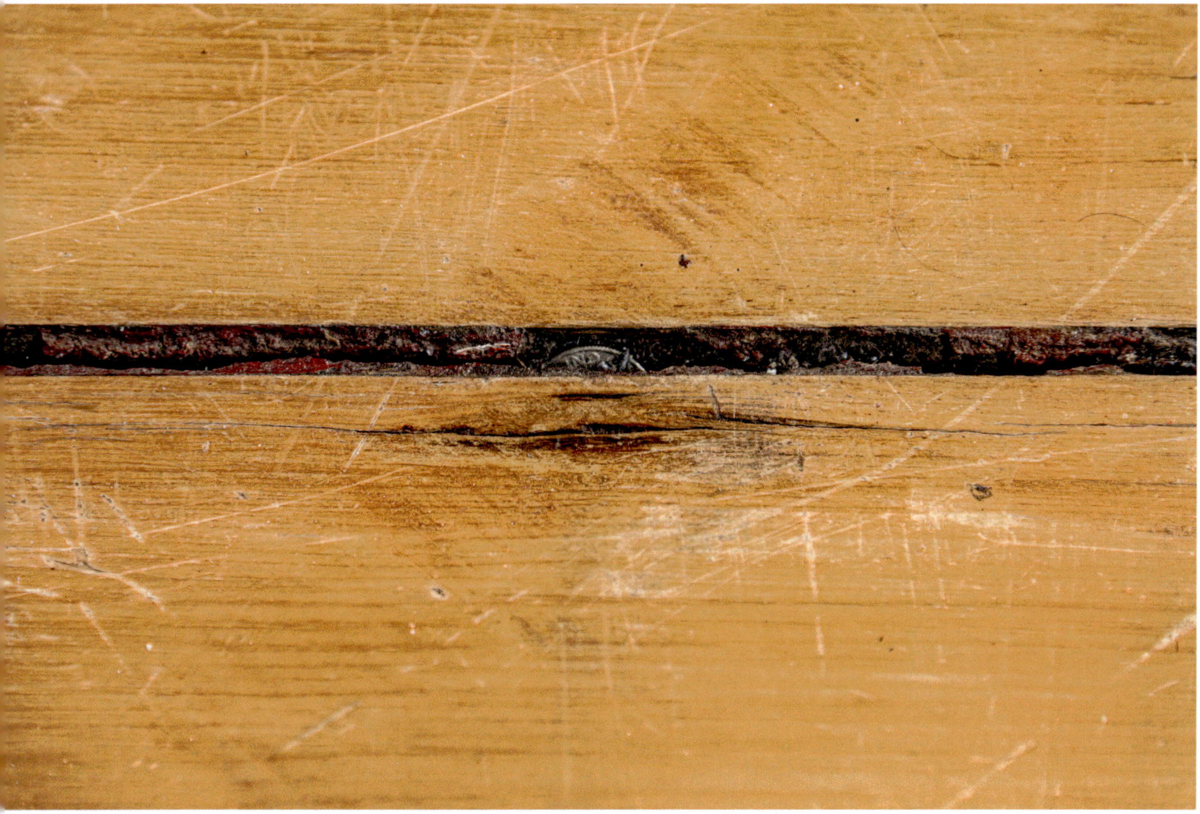

Is growth a must?

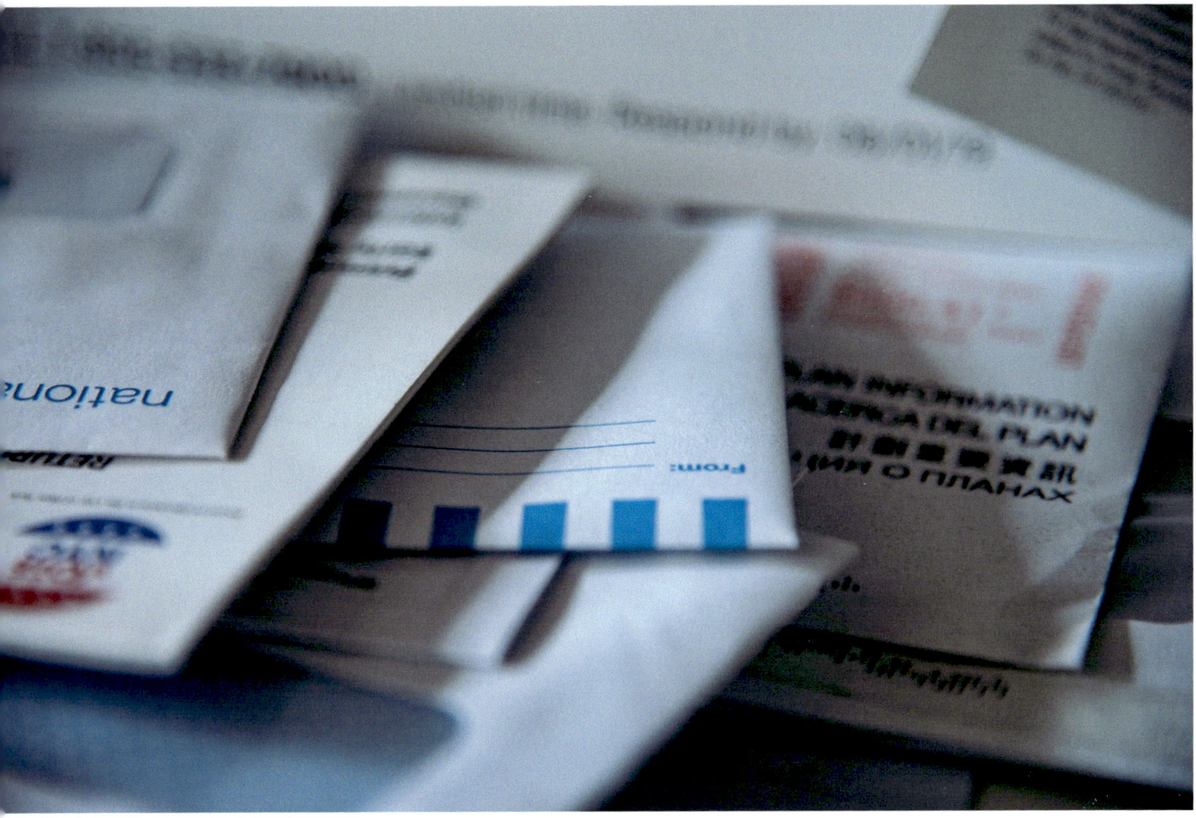

Will you live to see the changes for which you hope?

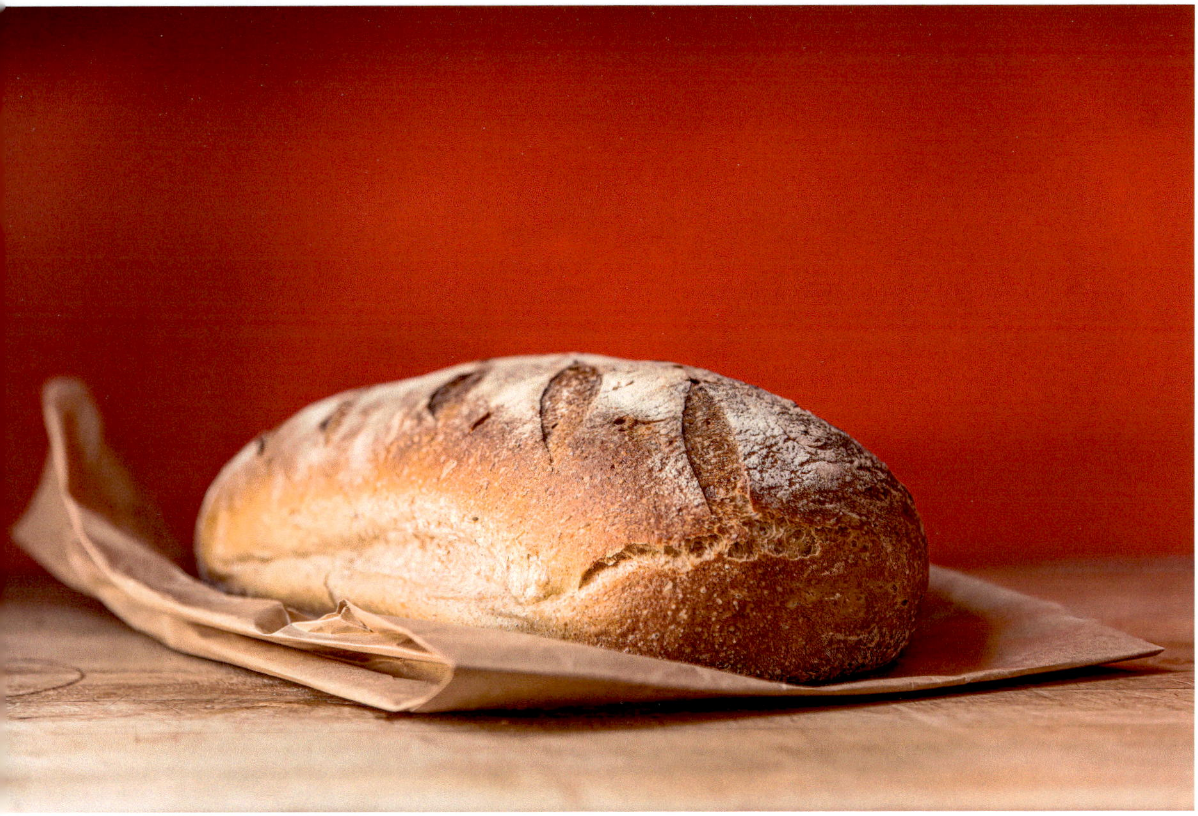

Are concessions gained by a sudden change of heart?

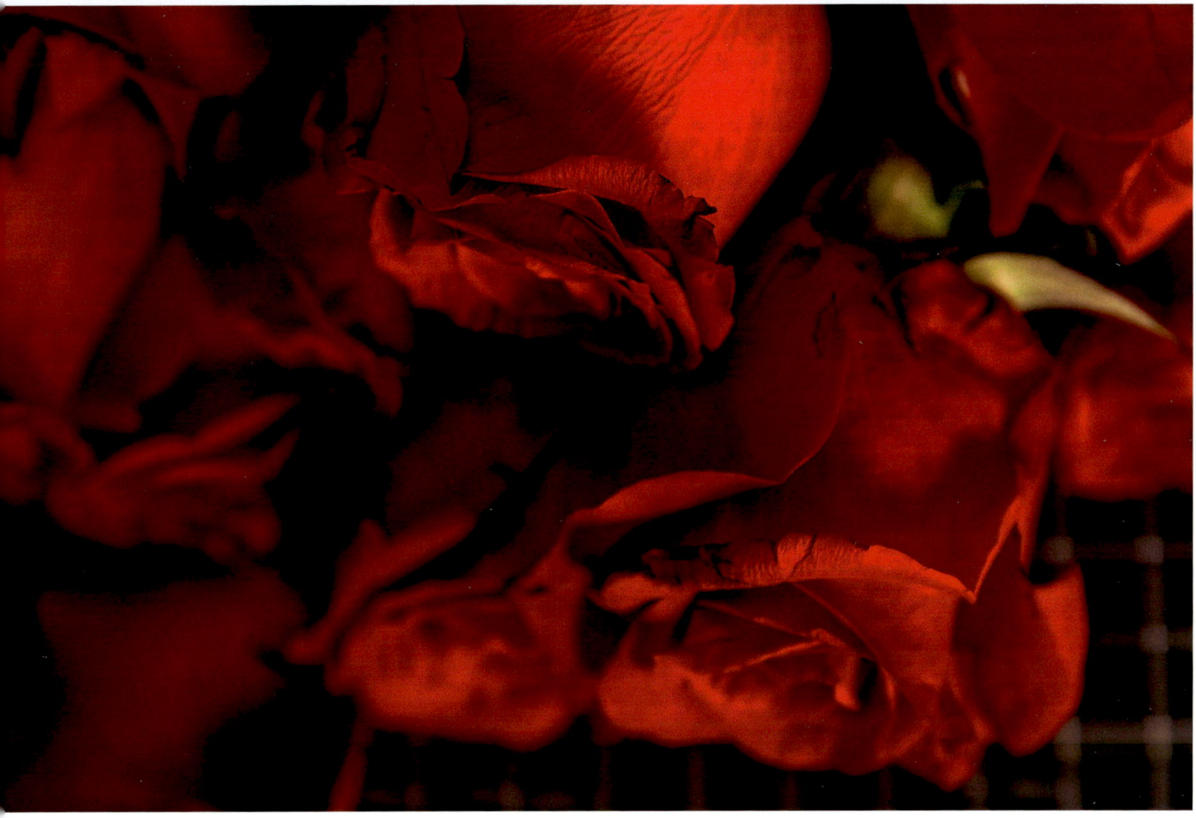

Is a choice decided a choice made?

In the following, I offer an interrogation of *homo economicus*; the world-historical, rational choice agent whose abstract individualism expresses the social form that turns life into a life lived for itself, in spite of itself. I attempt this through a montage of substitutions—premise for promise; the individual for the social; *you* for *us;* the "aw, shucks" of who you might be for the citizenry of who you should be; Mandeville's *Grumbling Hive* for Kant's *Kingdom of Ends*; the Vale of Tears for the Hidden Abode; etc. If austerity is a collective conviction that there is no such thing as society, rather only individuals, as subject matter, it provides a backdrop against which the individual as an ideal type whose central dilemma—to squander life for the sake of the living—may be exhibited as if it were *homo ethicus*.

The work splits itself in two: image and text. The images depict the built environment of that great ensemble of individuals, New York City. The text consists of brief questions addressed directly at *you*: a sovereign entitled to all the rights of alienation and appropriation adequate for a society realized by exchange relations. Obvious at first glance, the questions that accompany each image are not literal in the way that they might be in a questionnaire that seeks to position the relationship between art and its audience or one between an employer and an employee. Rather, these demands are pressed as an advertisement for life insurance might—an addressee is interpellated as a subject incomplete without the address that

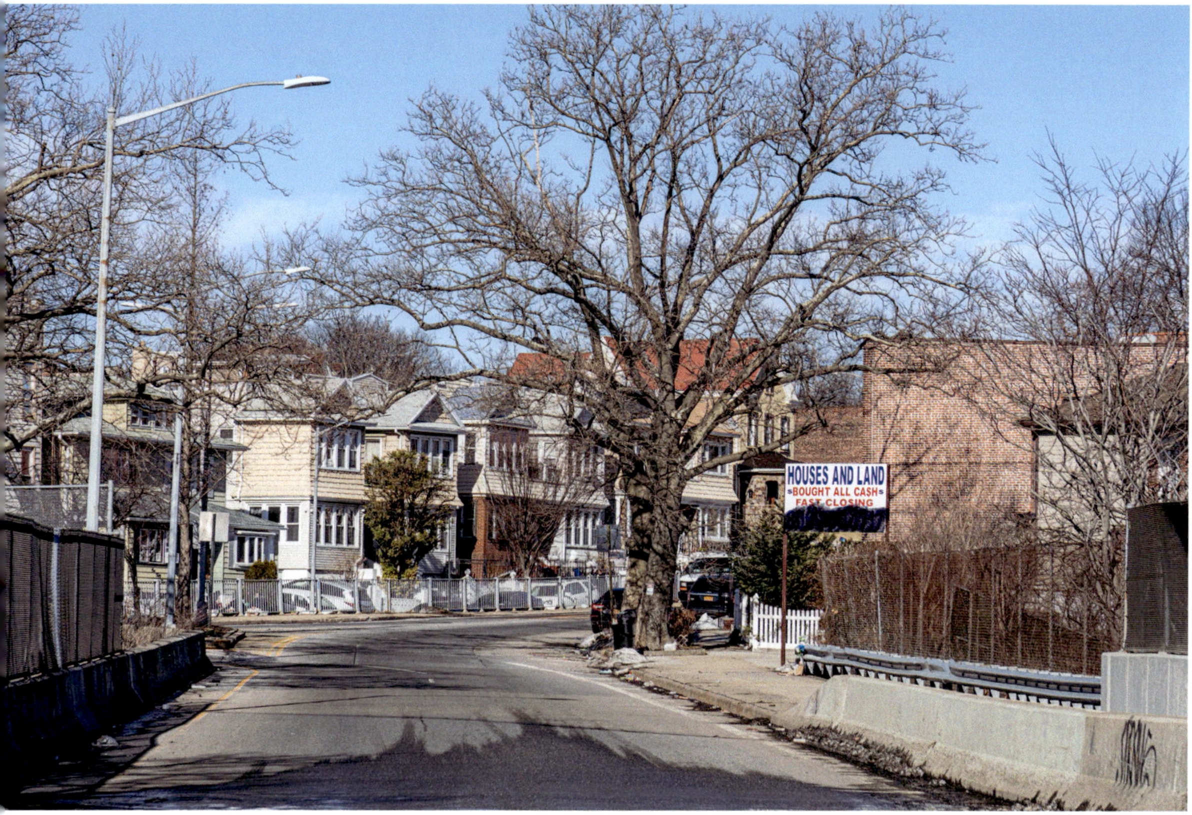

Can a ghost story frighten the one who tells it?

stands before them. Additionally, a promise of universal happiness is preserved at the moment that its implied absence is recognized. However, if this exercise of hegemonic demand were to be turned on its head, the question may end up antagonizing its viewer like the old marching anthem that demands to know, "Which side are you on?"

The premise of choice presents an individual with the possibility of irrationality—if not outright madness—at every juncture of this interpellative process. To an individual, there is no need to reconcile reason, the object of thought, with happiness, the object of utility. One typically settles for one at the expense of another. However, often enough the desire to harmonize the two prevails nevertheless. The rationalization of subjective interest into a public choice actor might be one abstruse way of articulating this overdetermination. This would interpret the calculation of individual self-interest as an expression of a *quid pro quo* common sense whose relative dominance positions non-compliance as the *de facto* essence of fools. The only rhetorical question included in this book attempts an example of this banal prohibition of refusal— "Why save when the value of your assets does it for you?" Otherwise, one can simply imagine a person struggling to keep their head above water as they go about their day.

Can an abstract individual and its liberty to choose but not refuse describe a social order that claims that "all are equal before the law" while in the same breath insists that "there is no entry except on business"? How might one respond to a demand that misrecognizes an individual property owner as an ideal social being? Rousseau outlines such a figure at the onset of *Emile*:

> One who wishes to preserve the sovereignty of natural feeling in civil society knows not what one asks. Ever at war with oneself, veering between inclination and duty, one can be neither an individual nor a citizen. One will be no good to oneself nor to others. One will be an individual of our times. One will be nothing. (1)

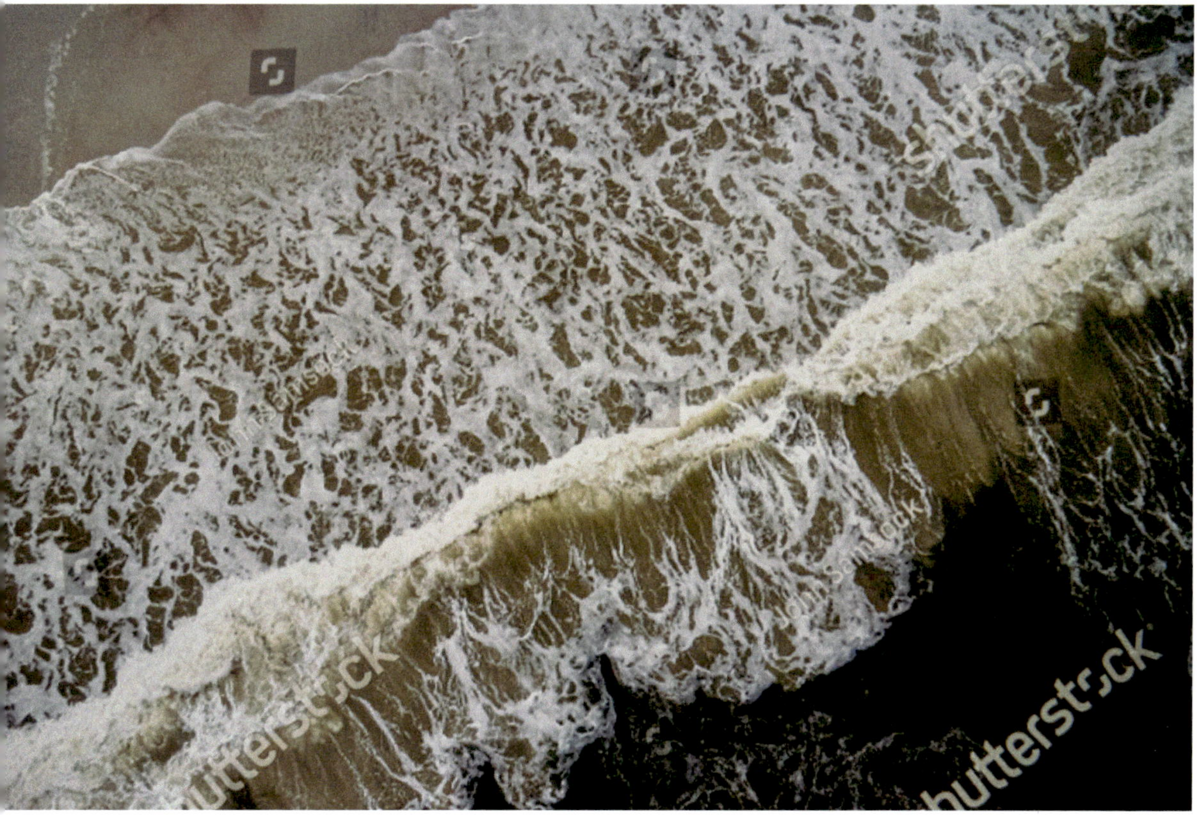

Have you yelled “Fuck the police!” at the police?

The photographic images deliver a similar ambiguity. As images of a particular place at a particular time, if a concrete reality is documented, it is by default alone. Instead, a generic reality is "chosen" as an image to the extent that it is photographically possible: life in a city as a phantom of life in *the* city; hallucination and dissolution in a metropolis that serves as a center for so much and, in doing so, centers so little. If catastrophe were ordinary, it would be sentimentalized into a stock image available for purchase.

Is there any cold comfort to be found in a scenic view that is a scene of crisis? If no two viewpoints were alike, from whose standpoint would crisis be recognized? As a struggle for recognition, would the identification of crisis function as a reflex of hegemonic self-interest? Is one necessarily safer when the profits are higher? Might the moment of crisis be relative for some, yet absolute for others? Reflecting on the economic depression of 1873-1896, Thorstein Veblen describes the hegemony of "the affections of the business men" in the following:

> Depression is primarily a malady of the affections of the business men. That is the seat of the difficulty. The stagnation of industry and the hardships suffered by other classes are of the nature of symptoms and secondary effects. Any proposed remedy, therefore, must be of such a nature as to reach this emotional seat of the trouble and restore the balance between the nominal value of the business capital engaged and the earnings of the business; that is to say, a remedy, to be efficacious, must restore profits to a "reasonable" rate. (2)

If one were to live in a rich man's world, would only those ends that satisfy his means suffice? Are the decisive moments of one's life the *Vorstellungen* of those for whom one's social being is otherwise marshaled? 60 years ago, Paul Samuelson's textbook example of market determination posits the market as the near-divine substance that manages a city like New York:

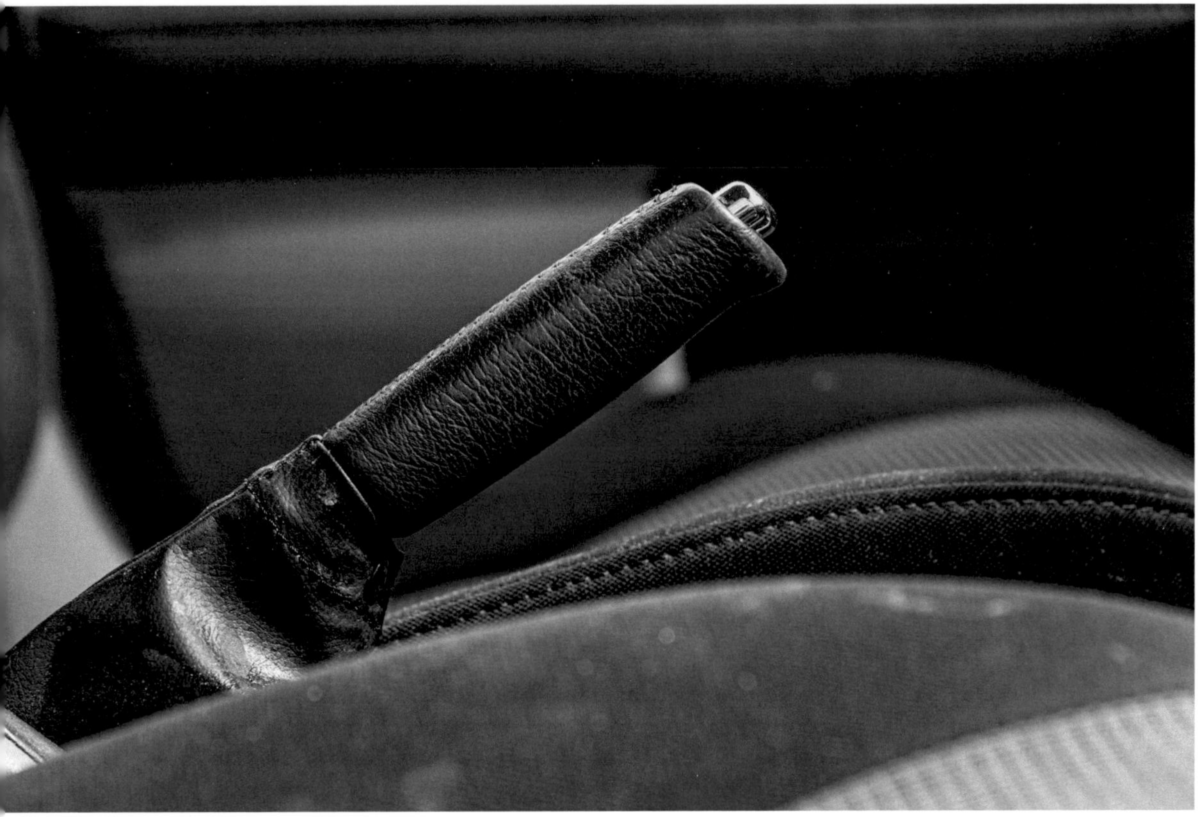

Have you thought “So, this is what it really looks like...” while cashing a check?

> How is it that nearly 10 million people in New York are able to sleep easily without mortal terror of a breakdown in the elaborate economic processes upon which the city's existence depends? For all this is undertaken without coercion or centralized direction by any conscious body. (3)

Nowadays, after the lessons of multiple bailouts, Samuelson's image of market-based social equilibrium hardly appears absolute. Only wishful thinking would imagine that the threatened expectations of the immediate and private interests formalized into a market as anything other than the consequence of massive political direction.

At the financial nadir of 2020's public health crisis, the mere promise by the US Federal Reserve to purchase non-financial corporate debt—that is, to act as a commercial bank that would socialize losses as a guarantee for private gains—was all that was needed to revive the corporate-bond-market bubble from which American corporations have skimmed their debt-financed earnings for years. And this is without the Fed having to even live up to its promise of moral obligation and buy a single bond. Self-interested private banks immediately renewed lending on the sole basis of a federal pledge to assure that none of their otherwise unprofitable clients would go belly up. The stock market soon followed suit. "We are all government-sponsored enterprises now" read one report as American bankers no longer bother to pretend that the market functions of its own accord. (4)

Might the subordination of the production of utility to the production of value root crises not in an economy's periodic vulnerability but in a persistent state of emergency suspended over, say, every resident of a cynosure of economic might like New York as if it were the sword of Damocles?

The city is not introduced, nor is it sent off, directly. The first and last images serve as indirect bookends to a project that otherwise remains within the five boroughs.

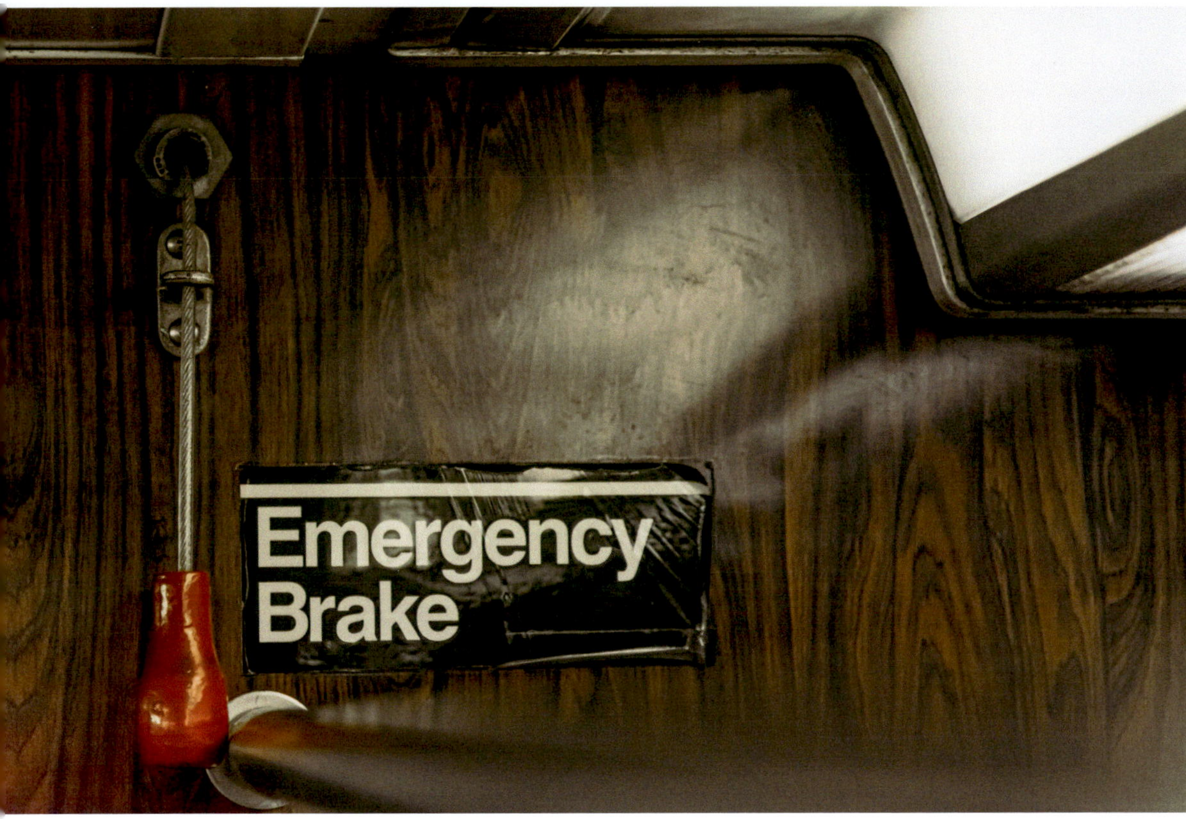

If you knew then what you know now, would it make a difference?

The first image depicts a highway at the edge of the American northern plains as a storm departs over a distant ridge. The image self-consciously panders to the communicative cliches of the previously mentioned insurance advertisements: a bend in the road comes to represent the mastery that one has exercised over the course of one's life. However, when taken for a documentary image and not a commercial hallucination, the image depicts the South Dakota state road to Wounded Knee Creek, the site of 1890 Wounded Knee Massacre, in which nearly 300 millenarian Ghost Dancers were slaughtered by U.S. soldiers. The memory of this act of carnage has defined this site as not only where the frontier came to an end but, after the American Indian Movement's 1973 occupation, as one of resistance—that is, to recall the popular phrase, a place to bury one's heart. Soon after this occupation, the term "frontier" found itself resurrected in the rhetoric that accompanied the postmodern redevelopment of devalorized and deindustrialized cities under the rubric of revitalization, marketing them as "new urban frontiers" for corporate "raiders" and yuppie "settlers." Understandable in relation to the concept of "accumulation by dispossession"—a slash-and-burn exploitation of the social power of money to forfeit the wealth of many into the hands of the few, a "frontier" such as New York City found itself remade into the packed market for speculative office space and luxury homeownership that it is today. An elaboration on the concept of primitive accumulation—the transformational act, historicized in letters of blood and fire, that inaugurates a capitalist mode of production, "accumulation by dispossession" grants significant power of explanation to the popular analogy that the conditions of contemporary urban existence are an afterlife of colonial conquest. Be it in criticisms of the draconian and ostensibly reformed "Broken Windows" and "Stop and Frisk" policies long practiced by the city's militarized law enforcement; practices that equated lawfulness with quality of life, underwriting discrimination as a state mandate to be enforced under the directive of "Zero Tolerance." Or, on the seemingly benign side of the spectrum, one might notice the commonplace practice of marketing cultural destinations in an underdeveloped neighborhood as an

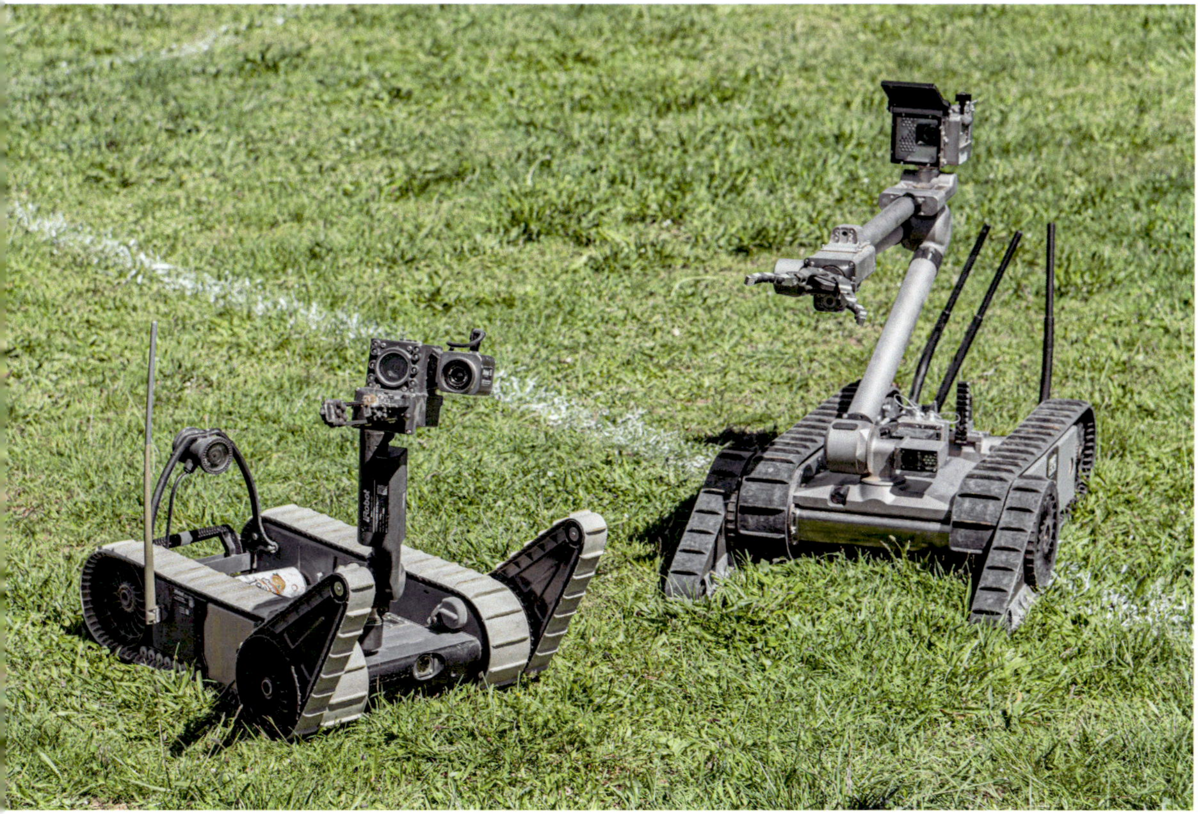

Do you identify with the culture into which you are nevertheless grouped?

"outpost" or of its recent residents as "transplants." Nevertheless, what is most important for the topic of an abstract individual is that this generalization of asset welfare as an austere form of public welfare individualizes one's right to the city as commensurate to what one can afford, establishing a pretext for predation by up-market actors and state-employed knuckleheads—that is, if one doesn't exercise the self-interest that seeks enlistment into the ranks of either. Displacement and flight thus become guaranteed "facts of life" that, until contested, dominate the horizon.

The concluding image was produced in reference to the title of this work and the exhibition of which it was a part. The title is a variation on the preliminary one that Ernst Bloch gave to his multivolume work, *Das Prinzip Hoffnung*—"The Promise of a Better Life." I came to learn that Bloch began this work while in exile from Nazi Germany, initiating its composition while residing in Marlborough, New Hampshire. The residence is since gone but a modest chapel contracted by its proprietors remains. The image depicts a bell hanging in an entryway beside the chapel, framing Mount Monadnock in the distance—a mountain whose Abenaki-derived name serves as an American equivalent to the Crusoe-esque geological term, *Inselberg*. "At the foot of the lighthouse is no light," reads a Bloch quotation in the image's title and the caption reads, "Will never enough make do?" Having recovered the concept of utopia for 20th-century thought, Bloch generalized its hermeneutic in the following passage:

> The morrow lives in today, and is constantly inquired after. The countenances that turned in the utopian direction have been different at different times. Yet the direction has everywhere been related, and actually, in regard to its still concealed goal, the same. Indeed, it appears to be the only constant in history. Happiness, freedom, non-alienation, the golden age, the land flowing with milk and honey—there are so many and diverse witnesses and pictures, yet all have but one focus, which speaks to us eloquently, notwithstanding its silence. The orientation to this evident focus must be invariant. This is recognizable wherever

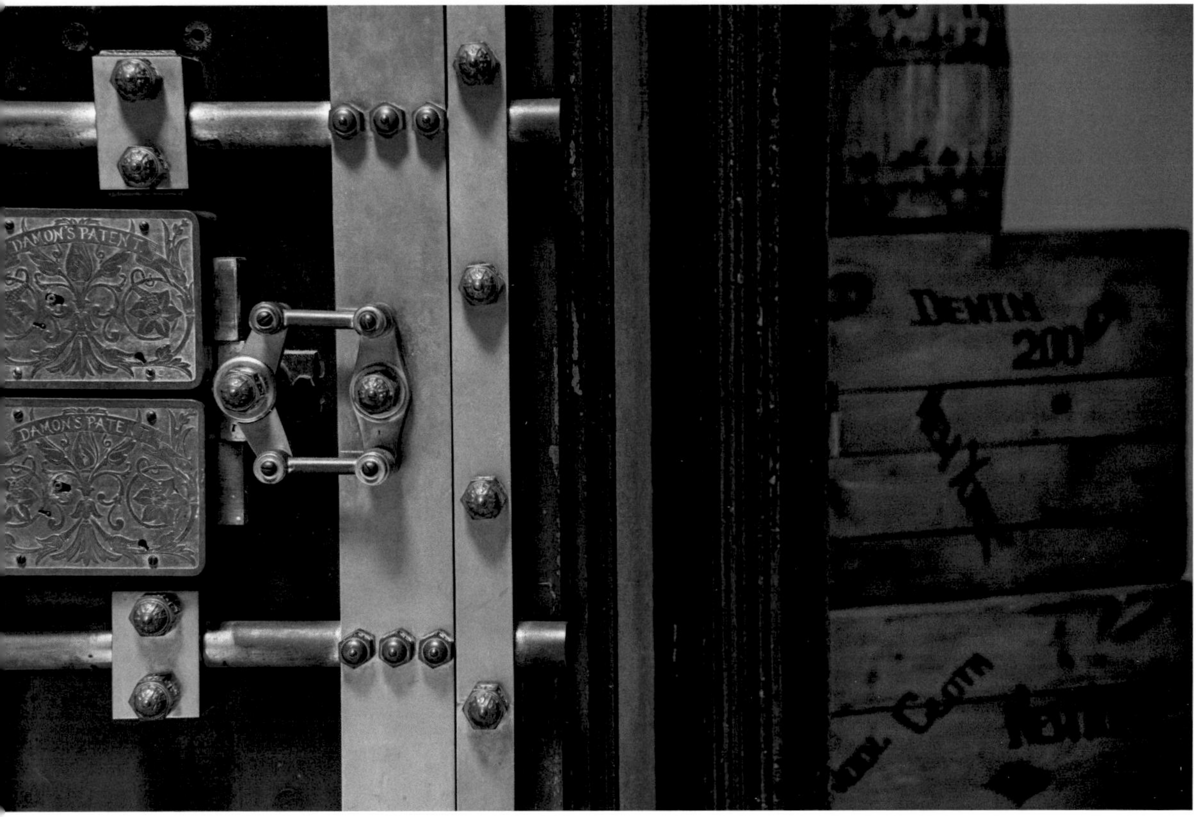

Is that which belongs to no one wasted by everyone?

> hope opens up its account and endeavors to read therein. There is never any doubt that an unilluminated, undirected hope easily leads some astray, for the true horizon does not reach beyond the knowledge of reality. But this knowledge, shows reality itself as a real horizon, and informed hope as congruous with such a reality. As the restless Abelard put it: "The goal is that community in which its desire does not precede its reality, and whose rewards are not less than such a desire." (5)

If utopia were to reside outside of history, its hope would operate within finite reality as it prepares the present to be other than what it is. It could be described as a silver linings routine, one that could slap a coat of paint on the initial cynicism of the claim, "there is no alternative," into an evident orientation that prepares a nation to "reach the other shore while groping at the stones underfoot." Another example might have the advertising slogan, "Act Now," become a militant call for direct action. While this may hazard consolation in the face of certain defeat (one will find Auden's famous words, "We are left alone with our day, and the time is short, and History to the defeated may say Alas but cannot help or pardon," elsewhere in this book), if a principle of non-identity were to condition a theory of utopia, its premise would be irreconcilable with its promise. That is, even if one doesn't know what one wants or needs, no one desires a broken promise. Thus, any failure of a better world to live up to reality forms utopia's next line of inquiry. No longer a fool's errand, utopia functions as a religion of everyday life built behind the back of that which would otherwise take us all for fools. At the conclusion of *The Principle of Hope*, Bloch claims that home is something that has never existed on this earth and that, for it to exist at all, it must first *not yet* exist. The images that introduce and conclude a presentation of what, for all intents and purposes, is the universal city aim to emphasize such a state of suspense.

Between one image that figures a flight from Egypt and another a road to Damascus, sinks a city on the hill, so to speak; a proverbial place whose image of home

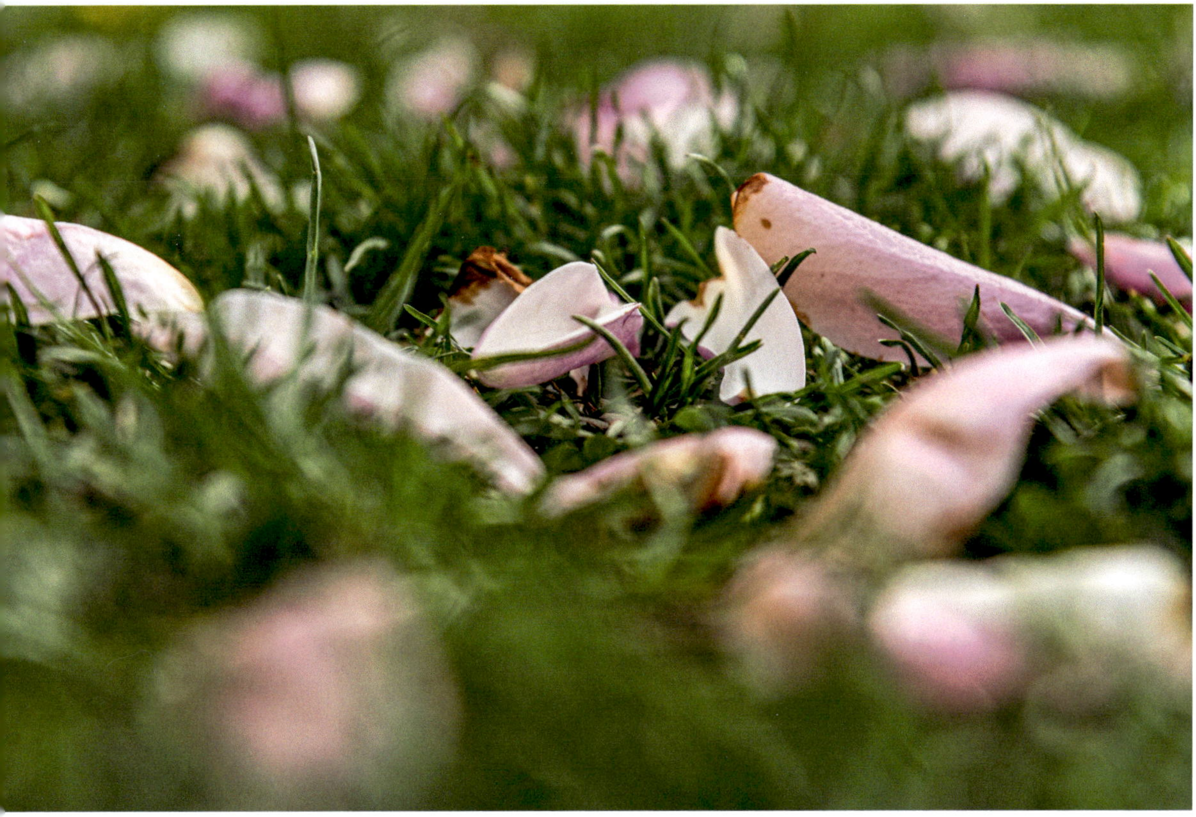

Would you bother changing if you weren’t counting on the returns?

coincides with an inalienable right to alienate and appropriate in an age of rising sea levels. It is the task of working through this right to commodity fetishism, of personally reckoning with the maddening world-historical effect of attributing infinity to the finite, of underwriting what appears at hand with the drama of whether an equivalent is stored in one's pocket, that serves as this project's eponymous premise. Daily scenes appear as if they were merchandise whose value was held in doubt. Real estate, institutional spaces, stock graphics, pedagogical charts, flora and fauna, and personal resolutions are conveyed as the popular attributes of an actually-existing life whose impossible universality settles on what appears generic. *The Premise of a Better Life* presents an imaginary of a residually modern society whose structure and history is never not out of joint, whose identity of unevenness and consolidation is never not ideal, substituting atavism for progress in a permanent restoration that would bulldoze achievement wherever it could not lay claim to it. Self-reckoning? Sure. An audit of the individual to see what it is about the concept to which to still cling? Ideally. As states face crises seemingly in excess of the economic, as pandemic and rising temperatures signal grim updates on the "sustainability" of human society, austerity as an image of governance has found itself under review. As a point of collision between GDP and population, scarcity has now returned as a topic of popular bluster for the globally dominant North Atlantic nations. This signals a decline in the fortunes of the individual as a figure of social interest and a renewed topicality for that singular possession, citizenship—the resume of *homo politicus*. This reconciliation with reality—that is, if normative community mistaken as a gift of nature were some sort of reality—more often than not stumbles into chauvinism, demography and the need to naturalize the former with the latter. As national defense budgets swell, the right to political community is taken as a substitute for the right to life and citizenry appears pegged to a global hierarchy of market magnitudes that mediate the world's finite resources as national entitlements patinated by an antiquated delusion of communitarian dispensation. Had I proceeded with some of

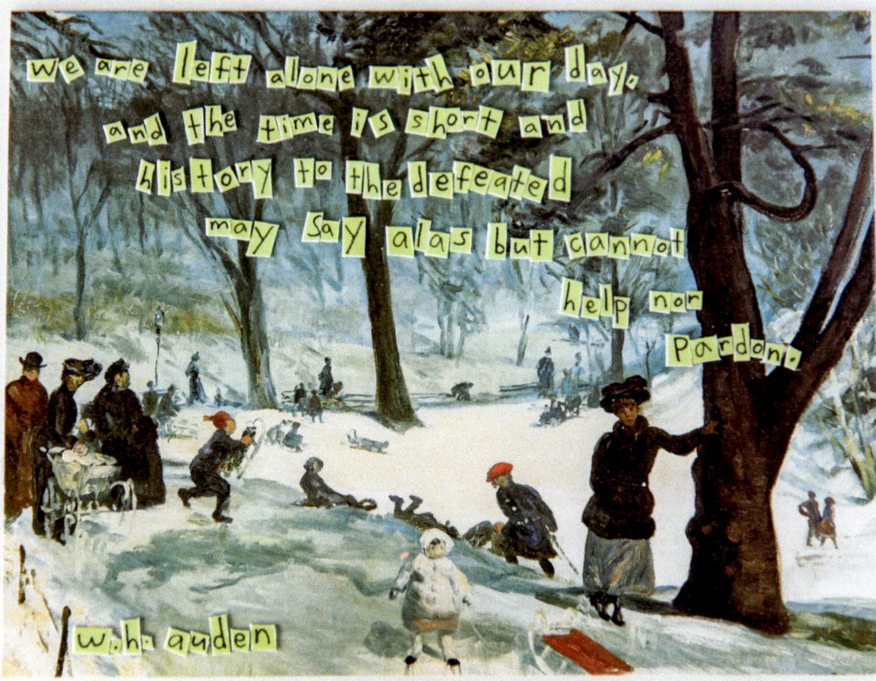

Is struggle more than just conflict?

the grim lessons of 2020 in mind, this project might have borne the even more miserable title, *The Premise of a Better Fate*.

Do these two halves—the individual and the city, text and image—add up to a whole? Of course not. What to make of a city symphony in an economy of evergreen crisis and a *mea culpa* for a person who exists only by premise alone? "Everyday life as the meaning of partisanship in mimesis" was Lukács' slogan for realism, which this work cannot or fails to be. Neither does it fit the aesthetic imperative of political abstention whose Cold War protest against instrumental reason (see Adorno and Marcuse *contra* Lukács) lingers in the present like the spoils of a pyrrhic victory. Beyond an accusation of dilettantism in part because of an apparent lack of either commitment or seriousness, would there be any benefit in offering artistic work that confers neither the spontaneous philosophy of the artist-activists nor the immediate results of the process of aesthetic autonomy? Damned if you do, damned if you don't? If it were better to fail nobly than to succeed basely, would the failure of one social form orient the possibility of another? The attempt that this work makes to articulate that which pits unequal parts—an individual and society—at irreconcilable odds is a wager such that it may pose this opposition as all the more trenchant in its attempt to appear ordinary. This is in no way an attempt to feign smug despair. Individuals are measurable by an equal standard only when brought under a single point of view. If an abstract individual were overdetermined as powerless, its lack of social agency would be demonstrative. One's real possibility in society—in concrete collectivity—would only be recognized by virtue of an invitation for critical negation.

If one were to take the time to answer any of the questions posed in this book, I doubt that those individuals subject to another's interests would answer in agreement with those whose needs have heretofore come to define interest as such.

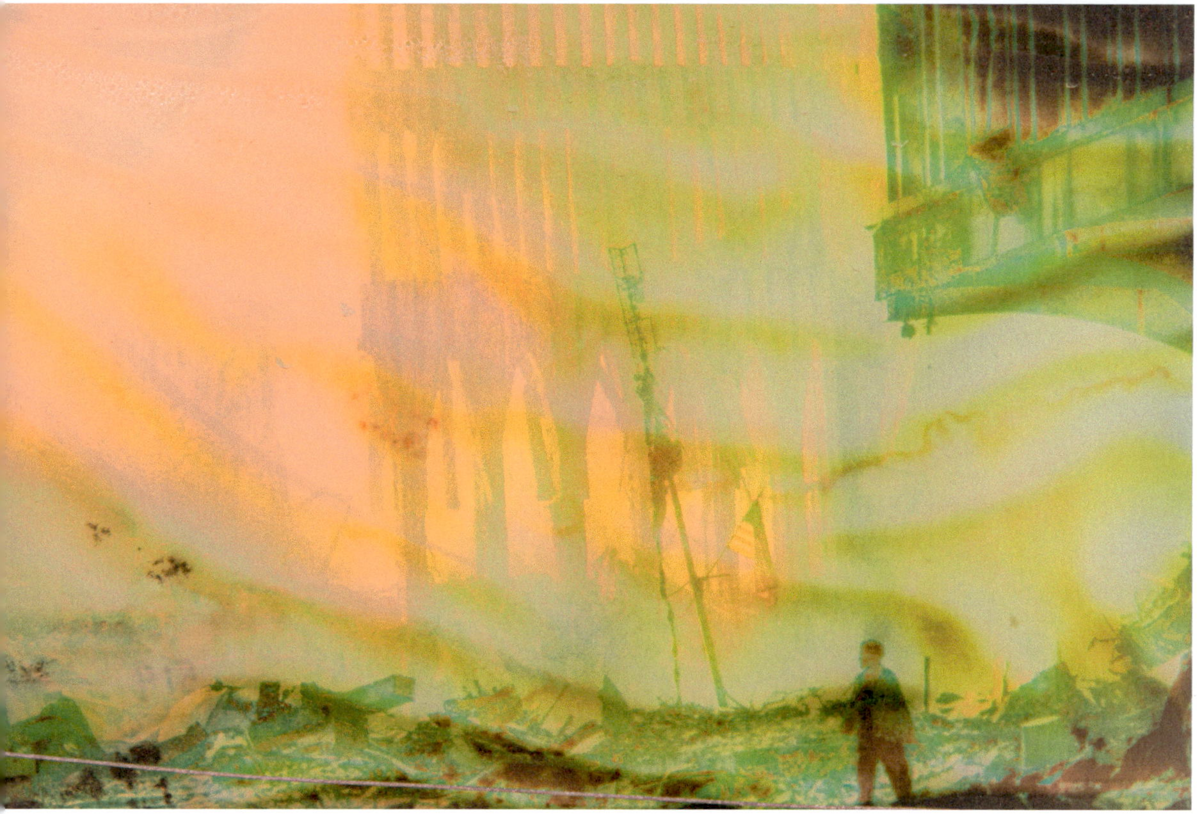

Do you exhibit the consequences of cheap lending and reppressed wage growth?

NOTES

(1) Jean-Jacques Rousseau, *Emile, or Education* (1762), tr. Barbara Foxley (London & Toronto: J.M. Dent and Sons; New York: E.P. Dutton, 1921), 8.

(2) Thorstein Veblen, *The Theory of Business Enterprise* (1904), ed. Douglas Dowd (New Brunswick, NJ: Transaction Books, 1978), 241.

(3) Paul Samuelson, *Economics* (New York: McGraw-Hill, 1948, 1961), 38.

(4) These lines are a paraphrase of Robert Brenner, "Escalating Plunder," *New Left Review*, 123, May/June 2020.

(5) Ernst Bloch, "Karl Marx and Humanity: The Material of Hope," in *On Karl Marx* (1968), tr. John Maxwell (New York: Herder and Herder, 1971), 43-44.

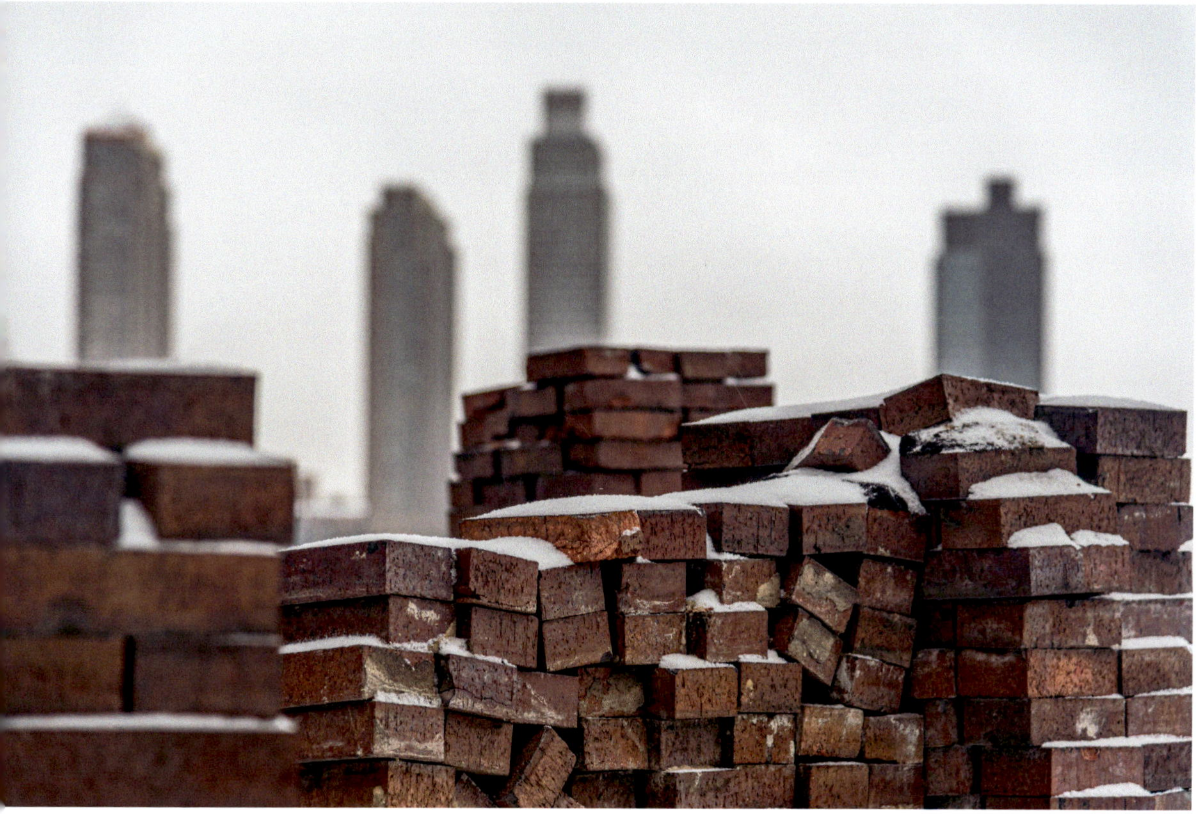

Are you safer when profits are higher?

Im Folgenden befrage ich den weltgeschichtlichen rationalen Entscheidungsagenten *Homo oeconomicus*, dessen abstrakter Individualismus jene Gesellschaftsform zum Ausdruck bringt, die das Leben in ein für sich selbst und trotz seiner selbst gelebtes Leben verwandelt. Ich versuche dies anhand einer Montage von Substitutionen: Prämisse statt Versprechen; das Individuelle statt des Gesellschaftlichen; *du* statt *wir*; die lokale Besonderheit, die du vielleicht bist, statt der abstrakten Gesamtheit, die du sein solltest; Mandevilles *unzufriedener Bienenstock* statt Kants *Reich der Zwecke*; das Jammertal statt der verborgenen Stätte der Produktion usw. Wenn die kollektive Überzeugung unter Austerität nun lautet, dass es keine Gesellschaft gibt, sondern nur Individuen, dann bieten diese als Gegenstand des Gesellschaftlichen einen Hintergrund, vor dem das Individuum als Idealtypus definiert wird, dessen wesentliches Problem es ist, das Leben um des Lebens willen einzuschränken, und dementsprechend als *Homo ethicus* auftreten könnte.

Die Arbeit ist in Bild und Text zweigeteilt: Die Bilder zeigen die erbaute Umwelt des grossen Ensembles aus Individuen, New York City. Der Text besteht aus kurzen, direkt an *dich* gerichteten Fragen: *Du*, eine Hoheit, die gemäss unserer durch Tauschbeziehungen verwirklichten Gesellschaft zu allen Rechten der Entfremdung und Aneignung befugt ist. Natürlich sind die Fragen, die jedes Bild begleiten, nicht so wörtlich gemeint wie in einem Fragebogen, der die Beziehung zwischen Kunst und Publikum oder zwischen

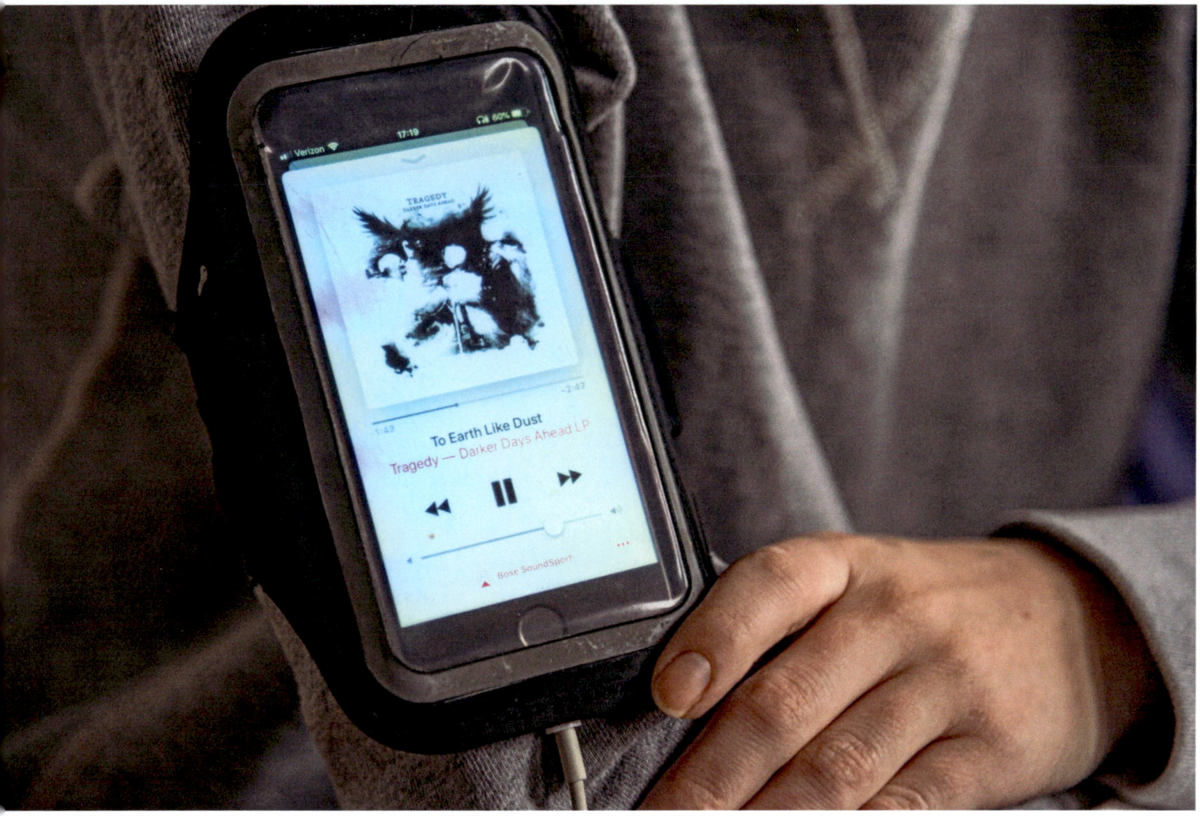

Do you exhibit the consequences of democratization and mass culture?

Arbeitnehmer:in und Arbeitgeber:in zu erfassen versucht. Vielmehr werden einem die Forderungen, welche die adressierte Person ohne vorhergehende Anrede als unvollkommenes Subjekt interpellieren, als eine Art Lebensversicherungswerbung aufgezwungen. Ausserdem bleibt das Versprechen von universalem Glück genau dann aufrechterhalten, wenn sein implizites Ausbleiben erkannt wird. Würden wir die hegemoniale Forderung auf den Kopf stellen, dann könnte die Frage ihr Publikum antagonisieren, wie die alte Marschhymne, die wissen will: «Auf welcher Seite stehst du?»

Die Prämisse der Entscheidungsfreiheit stellt das Individuum an jeder Stelle des Interpellationsprozesses vor die Möglichkeit der Irrationalität oder gar des Wahnsinns. Für ein Individuum ist es nicht zwingend, die Vernunft, den Denkgegenstand, mit Glück, dem Gebrauchsgegenstand, zu vereinbaren. Typischerweise entscheidet man sich für das eine auf Kosten des anderen, allerdings überwiegt der Wunsch, beides in Einklang zu bringen, doch meistens. Die Rationalisierung der subjektiven Interessen in einen öffentlichen Entscheidungsagenten könnte eine abstruse Art und Weise sein, diese Überdeterminierung zu artikulieren. Diese würde die Berechnung des individuellen Eigeninteresses als Ausdruck von *quid pro quo*-Denken, dessen relative Dominanz eine Missachtung als idiotische Handlung bezeichnen würde, interpretieren. Die einzige rhetorische Frage dieses Buches versucht ein Beispiel dieses banalen Verweigerungsverbots: «Warum sparen, wenn der Wert deines Vermögens dies für dich erledigt?» Abgesehen davon, kann man sich vorstellen, dass eine Person darum kämpft, den Kopf über Wasser zu halten, währenddem sie ihrem Tag nachgeht.

Kann ein abstraktes Individuum mit Entscheidungs-, aber ohne Verweigerungsfreiheit eine Gesellschaftsform repräsentieren, die behauptet, dass «alle vor dem Gesetz gleich sind», und im selben Atemzug darauf besteht, dass «nur ein geschäftlicher Weg existiert»? Wie könnte eine Reaktion auf die Forderung, die individuelle Eigentümer:innen als ideales gesellschaftliches Wesen missversteht, aussehen? Rousseau skizziert eine solche Figur zu Beginn von *Émile*:

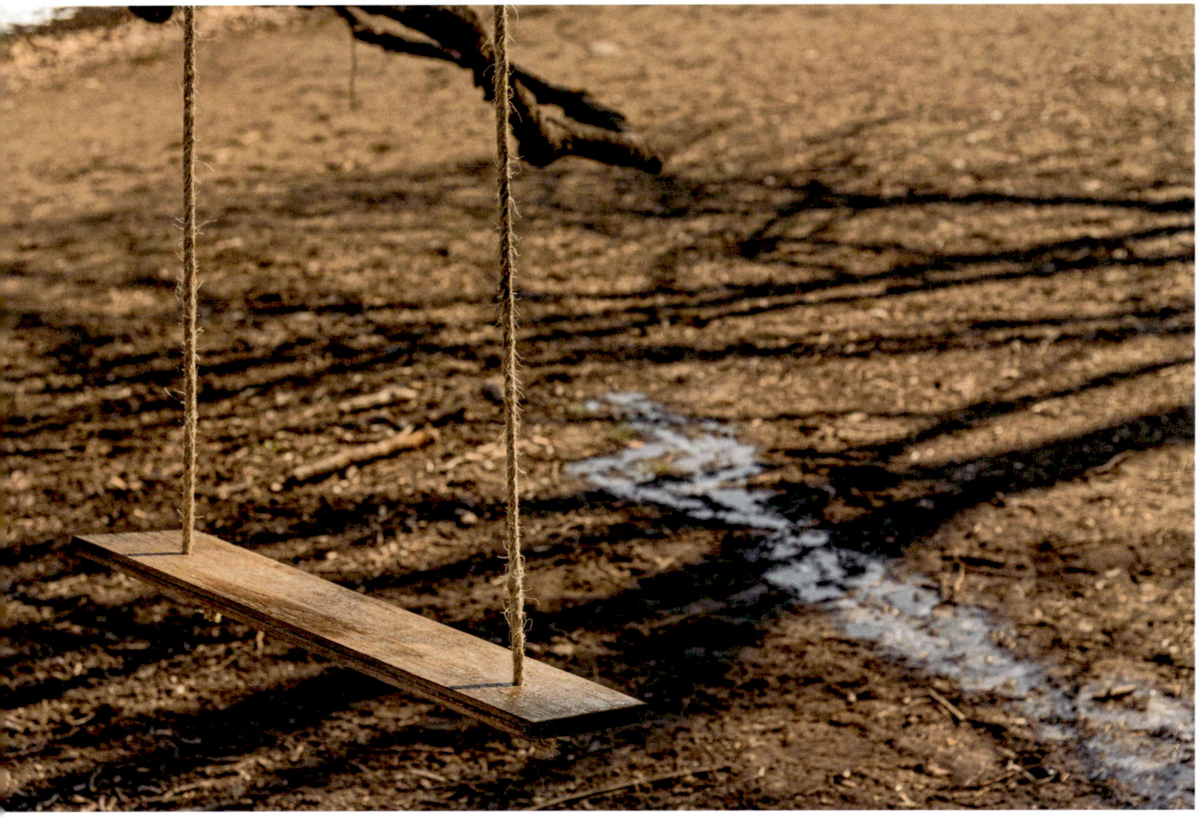

Do you keep your head when others lose theirs?

> Wer in der bürgerlichen Ordnung den Naturgefühlen den Vorrang einräumen will, der weiss nicht, was er will. Stets im Widerspruch mit sich selbst, stets zwischen seinen Trieben und Pflichten hin und her schwankend, wird er nie ein echter Mensch noch ein echter Bürger sein. Er wird weder sich noch anderen Vorteil gereichen. Er wird einer dieser Dutzendmenschen unserer Tage (...), er wird nichts sein. (1)

Eine vergleichbare Ambiguität vermitteln die fotografischen Bilder. Als Abbilder eines bestimmten Ortes zu einer bestimmten Zeit dokumentieren sie die konkrete Realität höchstens automatisch. Stattdessen wird eine generische Realität, soweit es fotografisch möglich ist, als Bild «gewählt»: ein Stadtleben als Phantom des Lebens in *der* Stadt, Halluzination und Verflüssigung in der Metropole, die als ein Zentrum für so viel dient und dabei so wenig konzentriert. Wäre eine Katastrophe alltäglich, würde sie zu einem verkäuflichen Stock Image verklärt.

Lässt sich Trost in einer Landschaft finden, die Schauplatz der Krise ist? Wenn zwei Perspektiven niemals dieselben sind, von welchem Standpunkt aus wäre eine Krise erkennbar? Würde die Identifizierung einer Krise als ein Reflex hegemonialen Eigeninteresses, als Kampf um Anerkennung funktionieren? Ist man sicherer, wenn höhere Gewinne erzielt werden? Ist der Moment der Krise für einige relativ und für andere absolut? Thorstein Veblen beschreibt in einer Reflexion der Depression der Jahre 1873-1896 die Hegemonie «der Neigungen der Geschäftsleute» folgendermassen:

> Eine Depression ist vorwiegend eine Krankheit der Neigungen der Geschäftsleute. Darin liegt die Schwierigkeit. Die Stagnierung der Industrie und die Not, die andere Klassen erleiden, sind der Ursprung der Symptome und Begleiterscheinungen. Deshalb muss jedes vorgeschlagene Mittel so beschaffen sein, dass es diesen emotionalen Kern des Problems erreicht und das Gleichgewicht zwischen dem nominalen Wert des eingesetzten Geschäftskapitals und den Erträgen des Geschäftes wiederherstellt. Dies bedeutet, damit ein Mittel effektiv sein kann, muss eine «angemessene» Profitrate wieder hergestellt werden. (2)

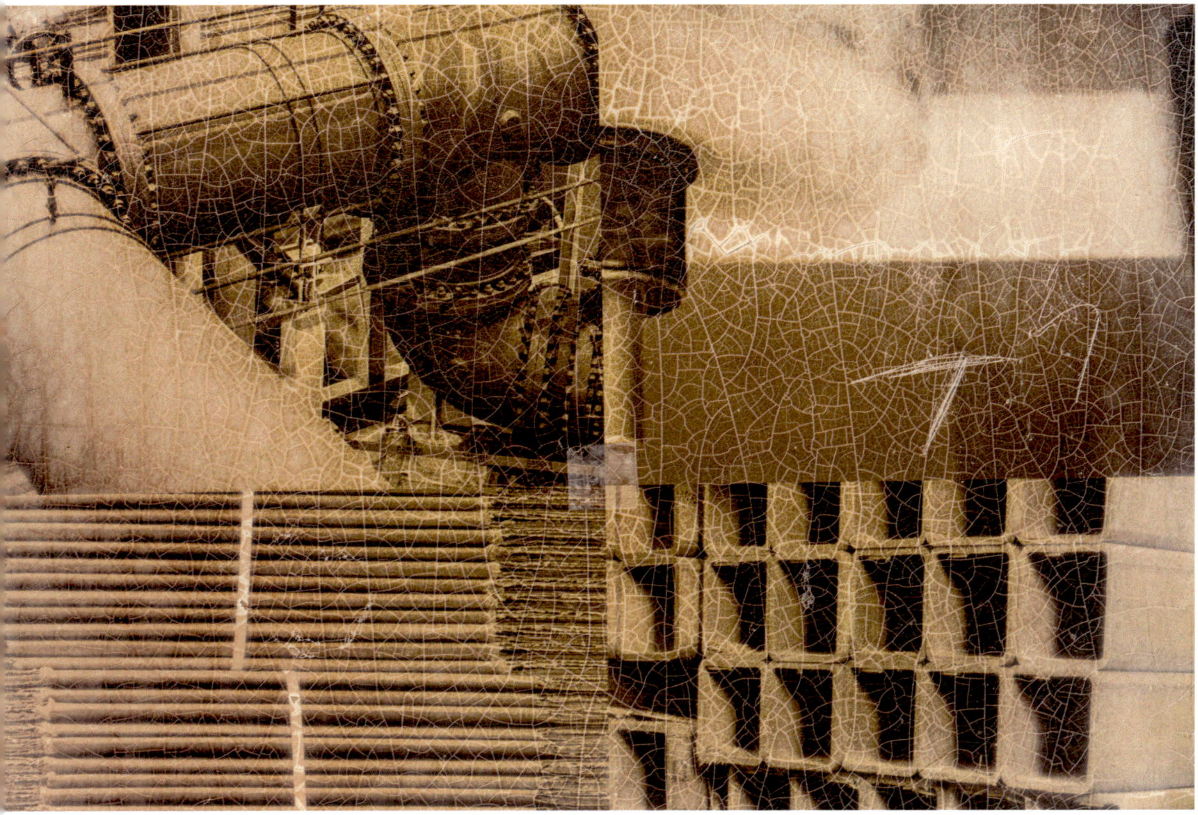

Are you first among equals?

Wenn man in einer Welt der Reichen leben würde, würden dann nur die Ziele verfolgt, die ihren Mitteln entsprechen? Sind die entscheidenden Momente deines Lebens die *Vorstellungen* jener, für die sonst dein gesellschaftliches Dasein eingesetzt wird? Vor sechzig Jahren postulierte Paul Samuelsons Lehrbuchbeispiel der Marktbestimmung, den Markt als eine nahezu göttliche Substanz zu sehen, die eine Stadt wie New York verwaltet:

> Wie ist es möglich, dass 10 Millionen Menschen in New York nachts ruhig schlafen können, ohne ständig mit Furcht und Schrecken an einen Zusammenbruch des komplizierten Wirtschaftsablaufs denken zu müssen, von dem das Leben der Stadt abhängt? Weil sämtliche damit verbundenen Tätigkeiten ohne Ausübung von Zwang oder zentraler Lenkung von irgendeiner Seite ablaufen. (3)

Nach zahlreichen finanziellen Rettungsaktionen erscheint Samuelsons Bild eines gesellschaftlichen Marktgleichgewichts heute kaum noch allgemeingültig. Es wäre reines Wunschdenken, die bedrohten Erwartungen der unmittelbaren und privaten Interessen, die den Markt ausmachen, nicht als Konsequenz einer massiven politischen Steuerung zu verstehen.

Am finanziellen Tiefpunkt der Gesundheitskrise im Jahr 2020 genügte ein blosses Versprechen der US-Notenbank, Schulden von Unternehmen ausserhalb des Finanzsektors anzukaufen – das heisst, als Geschäftsbank zu fungieren und Verluste als Garantie für private Gewinne zu verstaatlichen –, um die Blase des Marktes für Unternehmensanleihen, von der amerikanische Unternehmen seit Jahren ihre schuldenfinanzierten Gewinne abschöpfen, wiederzubeleben. Und dies sogar ohne dass die Notenbank das Versprechen ihrer moralischen Pflicht einlösen und eine einzige Anleihe kaufen musste. Die eigeninteressierten Privatbanken haben die Kreditvergabe sofort wieder aufgenommen und – dies allein auf der Basis der Zusage des Staates – dafür zu sorgen, dass niemand ihrer sonst unrentablen Kundschaft Konkurs geht. Der Aktienmarkt folgte bald darauf. «Wir sind jetzt alle staatlich geförderte Unternehmen», lautete ein Bericht, währenddem die amerikanischen

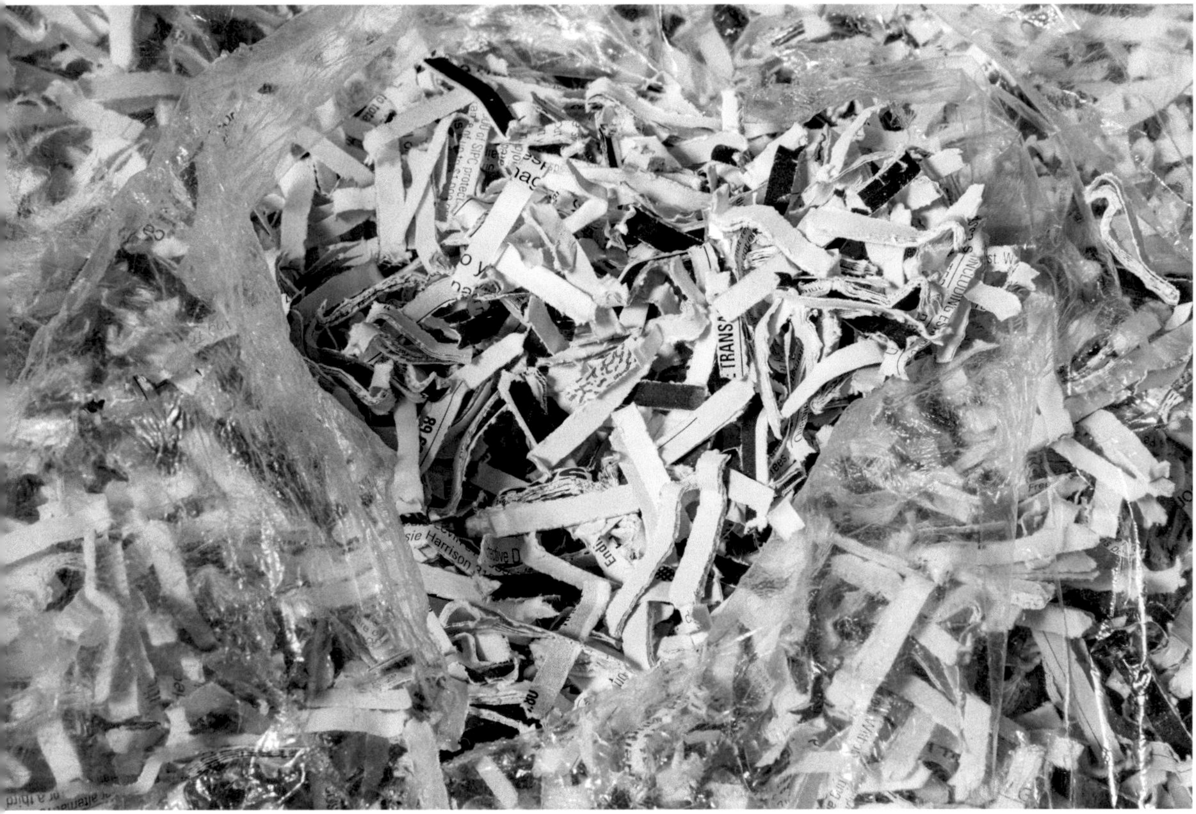

Is life without adventure not worth living?

Bankangestellten sich nicht mehr länger bemühten, so zu tun, als ob der Markt selbständig funktionieren würde. (4)

Verursacht die Unterordnung der Produktion von Nutzen unter die Produktion von Wert eine Krise, die nicht als periodische Wirtschaftsschwäche, sondern als andauernder Ausnahmezustand, sagen wir, wie ein Damoklesschwert über der Bevölkerung eines wirtschaftlichen Machtzentrums wie New York hängt?

Die Stadt wird nicht direkt vorgestellt, bleibt aber auch nicht anonym, obwohl sich ausser dem ersten und letzten Bild, die als eine Art Buchstütze des Projekts dienen, alles innerhalb der fünf Bezirke abspielt.

Das erste Bild zeigt eine Strasse am Rande einer nordamerikanischen Ebene, über deren Kamm in der Ferne ein Gewitter zieht. Das Bild bedient selbstbewusst die kommunikativen Klischees der bereits erwähnten Versicherungswerbung: Die Strassenkurve symbolisiert die erlangte Kontrolle über das eigene Leben. Wenn man das Bild jedoch als dokumentarisches Bild und nicht als kommerzielle Halluzination betrachtet, erkennt man South Dakotas Staatsstrasse Richtung Wounded Knee Creek, den Ort des Massakers von Wounded Knee des Jahres 1890, in dem nahezu 300 Geistertänzer:innen von US-amerikanischen Soldaten ermordet wurden. Die Erinnerungen an das Blutbad prägen den Ort nicht nur als Ort, an dem das «Grenzland» (engl. «frontier») aufgehoben wurde, sondern nach der Besetzung des American Indian Movement im Jahr 1973 als einen Ort des Widerstands – und einem volkstümlichen Ausdruck zufolge als Ort, an dem man sein Herz vergräbt.
Nicht lange nach der Besetzung tauchte der Begriff «Grenzland» in der Rhetorik, die den postmodernen Umbau entwerteter und deindustrialisierter Städte unter der Überschrift «Revitalisierung» begleitete und sie als «neues urbanes Grenzland» für aggressive Aktienaufkäufer:innen und Yuppie-«Siedler:innen» vermarktete, wieder auf. In Bezug auf das Konzept der «Akkumulation durch Enteignung», die brandroderische Ausbeutung durch die gesellschaftliche Macht des Geldes, den Reichtum vieler in die Hände der wenigen zu reichen, ist es verständlich, dass ein «Grenzland»

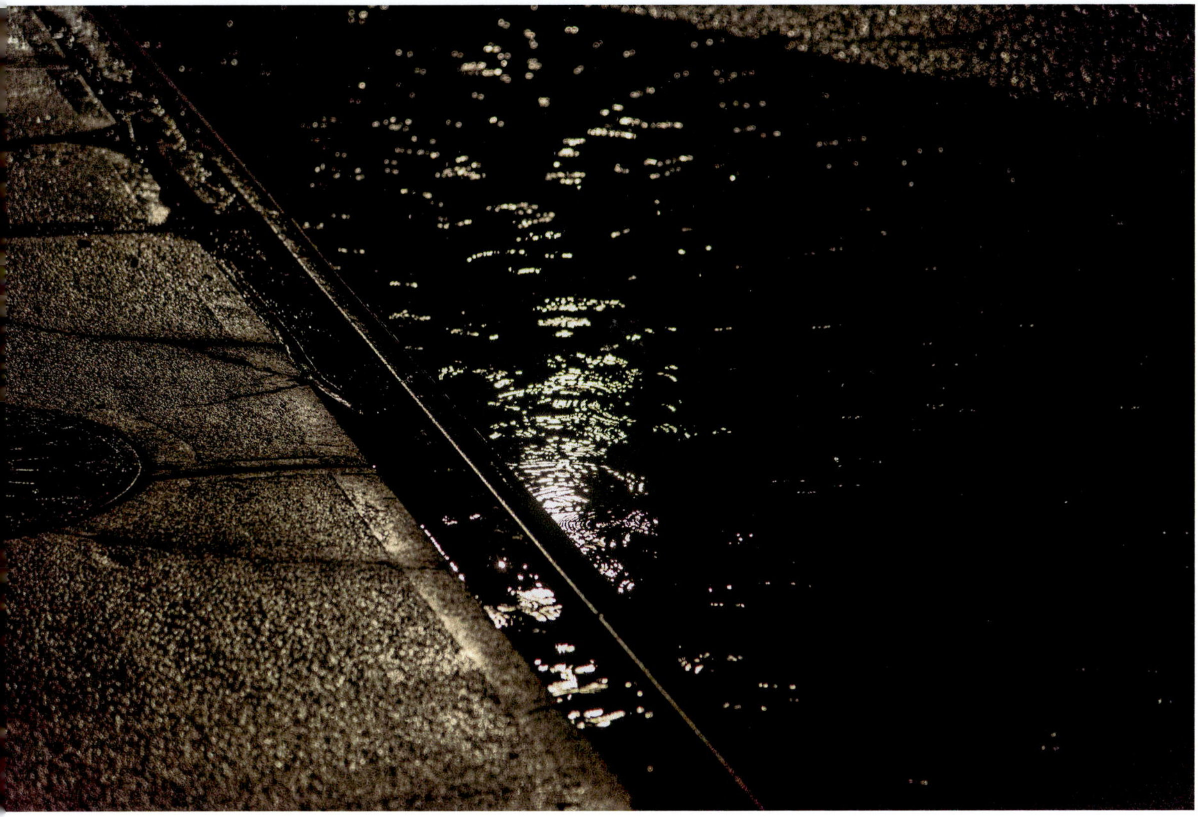

Is your well-being another's bottom line?

wie New York City zu dem komprimierten Markt für spekulative Büroflächen und Luxuswohneigentum wurde, der es heute ist. Eine Ausarbeitung des Konzepts der Primitiven Akkumulation, der transformative Akt, der die kapitalistische Produktionsweise ankündigte, ist in der Geschichte mit Blut und Feuer niedergeschrieben. «Akkumulation durch Enteignung» verleiht der gängigen Analogie, dass die Bedingungen der zeitgenössischen urbanen Existenz ein Nachleben der kolonialen Eroberung sind, erhebliche Erklärungskraft. Sei es durch Kritik am drakonischen, angeblich reformierten *Broken-Windows-* oder «*Stop-and-Frisk*»-Konzepts, das der militarisierte Gesetzesvollzug in der Stadt lange ausübte, Praktiken, die Rechtmässigkeit mit Lebensqualität gleichsetzen und Diskriminierung mit einer Nulltoleranzstrategie als Staatsauftrag durchsetzen. Oder auf der scheinbar harmlosen Seite des Spektrums könnte beobachtet werden, wie kulturelle Anziehungspunkte in einer unterentwickelten Nachbarschaft als «Aussenposten» und ihre jüngste Bevölkerung als «Transplantation» vermarktet werden. Was jedoch für das Thema eines abstrakten Individuums am wichtigsten ist, ist die Tatsache, dass diese Verallgemeinerung der Vermögenswohlfahrt als strenge Form der öffentlichen Wohlfahrt das eigene Recht auf die Stadt als gemessen an dem, was man sich leisten kann, individualisiert und einen Vorwand für die Ausbeutung durch gehobene Akteur:innen und staatlich angestellte Schwachköpfe schafft — das heisst, sofern man nicht aus Eigeninteresse die Aufnahme in die Reihen eines der beiden anstrebt. Vertreibung und Flucht werden so zu garantierten «Lebensfakten» und beherrschen, solange sie nicht bestritten werden, den Horizont.

Das abschliessende Bild wurde in Referenz zum Titel der Arbeit und der Ausstellung, in der sie gezeigt wurde, produziert. Der Titel *The Promise of a Better Life* («Die Hoffnungsprämisse») ist eine Variation des bereits erwähnten, mehrbändigen Werks von Ernst Bloch *Das Prinzip Hoffnung*. Wie ich erfahren habe, nahm Bloch die Komposition dieses Werks während seines Aufenthalts in Marlborough, New Hampshire, im Exil von Nazi-Deutschland auf. Das Haus steht inzwischen nicht mehr, aber eine bescheidene Kapelle, die die ehemaligen Eigentümer:innen errichteten, wurde

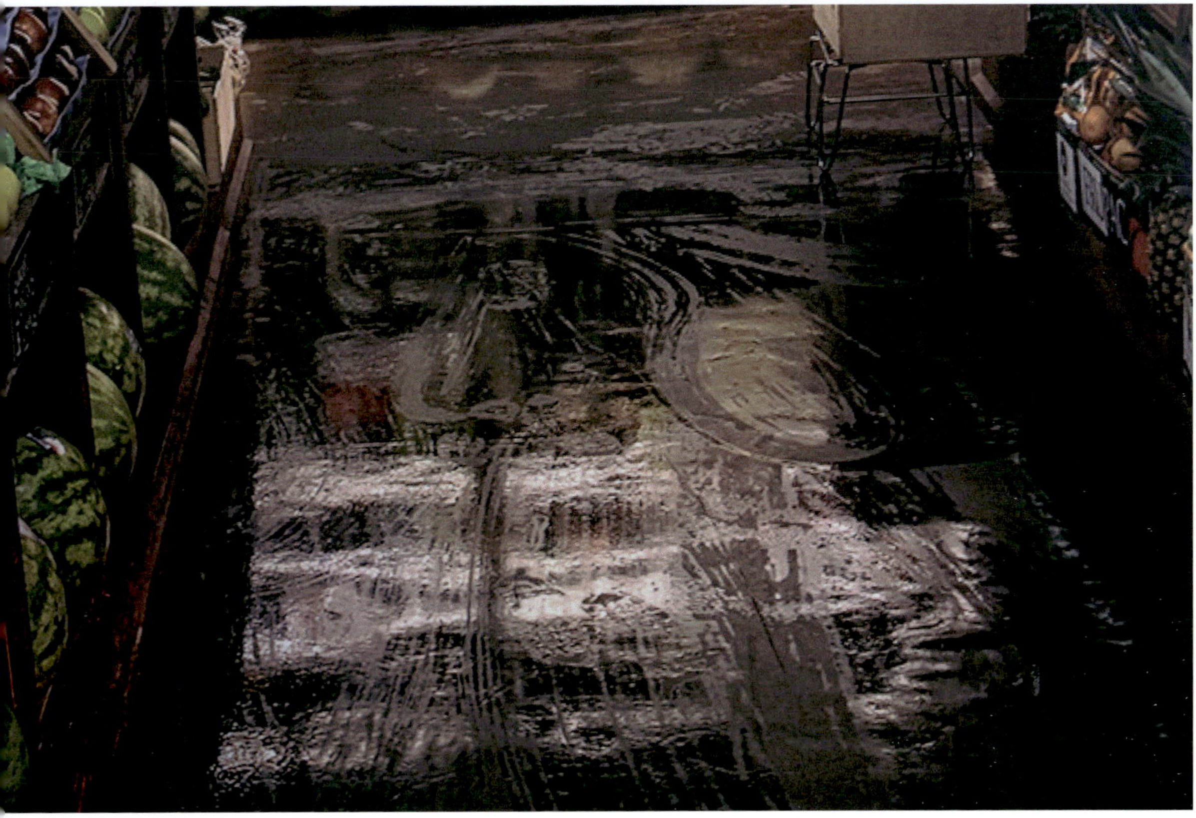

Have you been the excuse for someone else's atrocity?

erhalten. Das Bild zeigt eine herabhängende Glocke in einem Durchgang vor der Kapelle, die Mount Monadnock in der Ferne einrahmt - ein Berg, dessen Namen von den Abenaki abstammt und als amerikanisches Äquivalent des Crusoe-esken geologischen Ausdrucks *Inselberg* dient. «Am Fusse des Leuchtturms ist es dunkel», besagt ein Bloch-Zitat im Titel des Bildes, und die Bildunterschrift dazu lautet: «Wird nie genug reichen?» Bloch rehabilitierte das Konzept der Utopie für das Denken des 20. Jahrhunderts und verallgemeinerte dessen Hermeneutik in der folgenden Passage:

> Das Morgen im Heute lebt, es wird immer nach ihm gefragt. Die Gesichter, die sich in die utopische Richtung wandten, waren zu jeder Zeit verschieden (...). Die Richtung dagegen ist hier überall verwandt, ja in ihrem noch verdeckten Ziel die gleiche: Sie erscheint als das einzig Unveränderliche in der Geschichte. Glück, Freiheit, Nicht-Entfremdung, Goldenes Zeitalter, Land, wo Milch und Honig fliesst (...) es sind so viele und verschiedenwertige Zeugen und Bilder, doch alle um das her aufgestellt, was für sich selber spricht, indem es noch schweigt. Die Richtung auf dies materiell und nicht nur logisch Einleuchtende muss invariant sein; das ist an jedem Ort erkennbar, wo Hoffnung ihr Überhaupt aufschlägt und darin zu lesen versucht. Kein Zweifel allemal (...): eine unerhellte, ungelenkte Hoffnung führt leicht nur abseits, denn der wahre Horizont reicht nicht über die Erkenntnis der Realitäten, aber gerade diese Erkenntnis (...) zeigt die Realität selber als eine des Horizonts und die informierte Hoffnung als eine dieser Realität gemässe. (...) [Wie es] der unruhige Scholastiker Abälard [sagt] (...), Ziel ist jene Gemeinschaft, wo die Sehnsucht der Sache nicht zuvorkommt, noch die Erfüllung geringer ist als die Sehnsucht. (5)

Wenn die Utopie ausserhalb der Geschichte ansässig wäre, dann würde ihre Hoffnung innerhalb der endlichen Realität walten und die Gegenwart dazu vorbereiten, anders zu sein als das, was sie ist. Sie könnte als Glück im Unglück bezeichnet werden und dem anfänglichen Zynismus der Forderung «there is no alternative» (dt. «es gibt keine Alternative») einen neuen Anstrich verpassen und in der offensichtlichen Ausrichtung

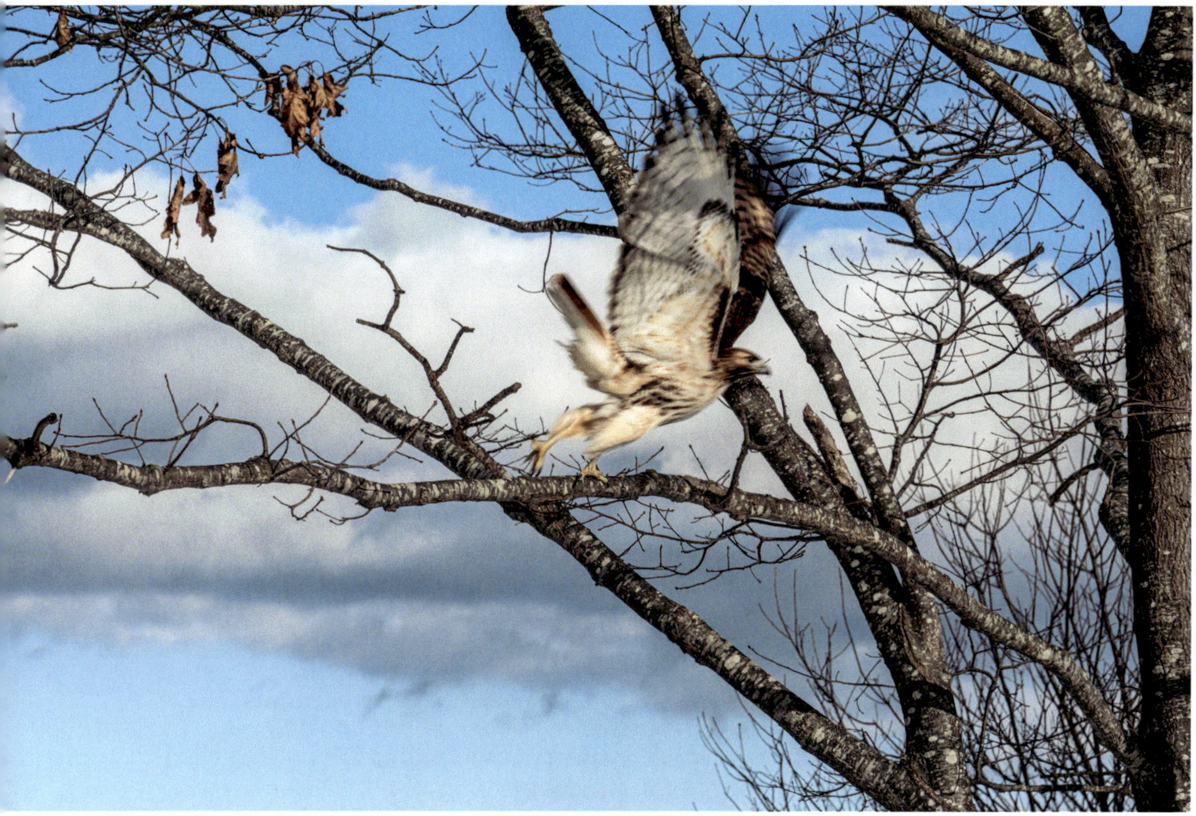

Are your hopes another's legacy?

münden, die eine Nation dazu vorbereitet, «das andere Ufer zu erreichen, während die Füsse über die Steine tasten». Ein anderes Beispiel ist der Werbeslogan, der zum militanten Aufruf für Protestaktionen wurde: «Act Now» (dt. «Jetzt handeln!»). Auch wenn dies angesichts der sicheren Niederlage ein Trost sein mag (Audens berühmte Worte sind an einer anderen Stelle in diesem Buch zu finden: «Wir sind alleine gelassen mit unserem Tag, und die Zeit ist kurz, und die Geschichte könnte zu den Bezwungenen sagen, Ach, aber kann nicht helfen oder begnadigen.»), würde ein Konzept der Nicht-Identität die Theorie der Utopie bestimmen, wäre die Prämisse mit ihrem Versprechen unvereinbar. Das heisst, selbst wenn man nicht weiss, was man will und braucht, wünscht sich niemand ein gebrochenes Versprechen. Folglich definiert jedes Scheitern einer besseren Welt an der Realität den nächsten Ansatzpunkt der Utopie. Die Utopie fungiert nicht mehr als Irrweg, sondern als Alltagsreligion, die hinter dem Rücken derer errichtet wird, die uns sonst für dumm verkaufen. In der Konklusion von *Das Prinzip Hoffnung* behauptet Bloch, dass Heimat auf dieser Welt nie existiert hat und damit sie je existieren kann, zunächst *noch nicht* existiert haben muss. Die einleitenden und abschliessenden Bilder der Präsentation, der im Grunde genommen universellen Stadt, zielen darauf ab, ein solches Spannungsfeld zu verdeutlichen.

Zwischen einem Bild, das die Flucht aus Ägypten und einen anderen Weg nach Damaskus zeigt, versinkt eine Stadt sozusagen auf dem Hügel; ein sprichwörtlicher Ort, dessen Vorstellung von Heimat mit dem unveräusserlichen Recht auf Entfremdung und Aneignung, im Zeitalter des Anstieges des Meeresspiegels, zusammenfällt. Die Aufgabe, dieses Recht zum Warenfetischismus aufzuarbeiten, persönlich mit dem verrückten weltgeschichtlichen Effekt abzurechnen, das Endliche dem Unendlichen zuzuschreiben, was greifbar erscheint, mit dem Drama zu unterlegen, und ob man ein Äquivalent in der Hosentasche finden kann, ist die namensgebende Prämisse dieses Projekts. Tägliche Szenen erscheinen als Ware, deren Wert angezweifelt wird. Immobilien, institutionelle Räume, Aktiengrafiken, pädagogische Diagramme, Flora und Fauna und persönliche Vorsätze

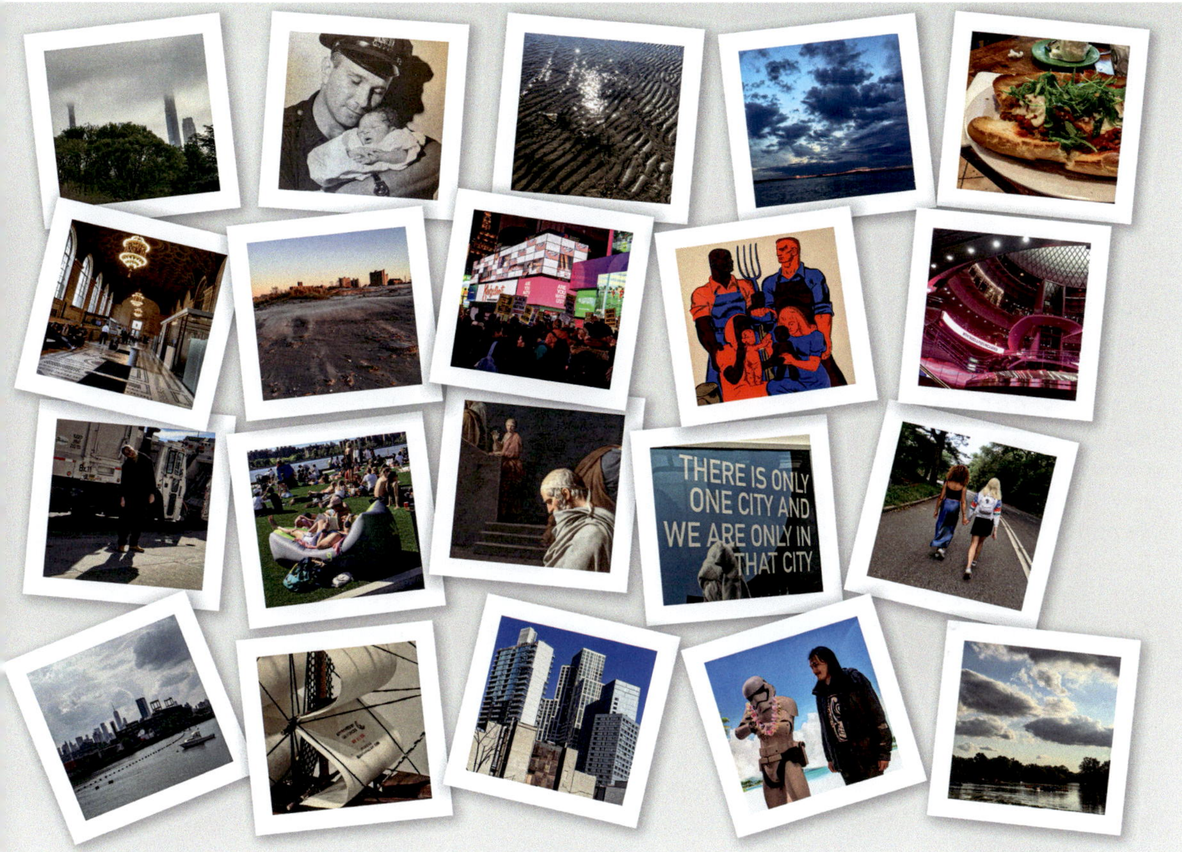

Do you tolerate a margin of loss for the sake of gain elsewhere?

werden einem als gängige Attribute eines real existierenden Lebens vermittelt, dessen unmögliche Allgemeingültigkeit sich auf das scheinbar Gewöhnliche niederschlägt. *Die Hoffnungsprämisse* entwirft das Imaginäre einer residuellen modernen Gesellschaft, deren Struktur und Geschichte niemals nicht aus den Fugen gerät, deren Identität aus Ungleichheit und Konsolidierung niemals nicht ideal ist und Atavismus mit Fortschritt in einem permanenten Erneuerungsprozess ersetzt und die nicht beanspruchbaren Errungenschaften niederwälzt. Selbstabrechnung? Klar. Ein Testen des Individuums, um herauszufinden, was an dem Konzept dran ist, an dem man immer noch festhält? Idealerweise. In einer Zeit, in der Staaten mit Krisen konfrontiert sind, die scheinbar über das Wirtschaftliche hinausgehen, in der die Pandemie und die steigenden Temperaturen düstere Signale für die «Nachhaltigkeit» der menschlichen Gesellschaft aussenden, steht die Austerität als Regierungsmodell auf dem Prüfstand. Als Kollisionspunkt zwischen BIP und Bevölkerung ist Knappheit nun wieder ein Thema geworden, über das die weltweit dominierenden nordatlantischen Nationen gerne toben. Dies ist ein Zeichen dafür, dass das Individuum als Figur des gesellschaftlichen Interesses an Bedeutung verliert und dass das einzigartige Eigentum, die Staatsbürger:innenschaft, wieder an Aktualität gewinnt – die Fortsetzung des *Homo politicus*. Diese Versöhnung mit der Realität – wenn die normative Gemeinschaft, die fälschlicherweise als Geschenk der Natur angesehen wird, eine Art Realität wäre – stösst häufig auf Chauvinismus, Demografie und die Notwendigkeit, das Erstere mit dem Letzteren zu neutralisieren. Während die nationalen Verteidigungsbudgets wachsen, wird das Recht auf politische Gemeinschaft als Ersatz für das Recht auf Leben angesehen, und die Bevölkerung scheint an die globale Hierarchie von Marktgrössen gekoppelt, welche die endlichen Ressourcen als nationale Ansprüche, die mit einer antiquierten Illusion der kommunitären Verteilung patiniert sind, vermittelt. Hätte ich einige der düsteren Lektionen des Jahres 2020 im Hinterkopf gehabt, hätte dieses Projekt den noch unglücklicheren Titel *Die Schicksalsprämisse* getragen.

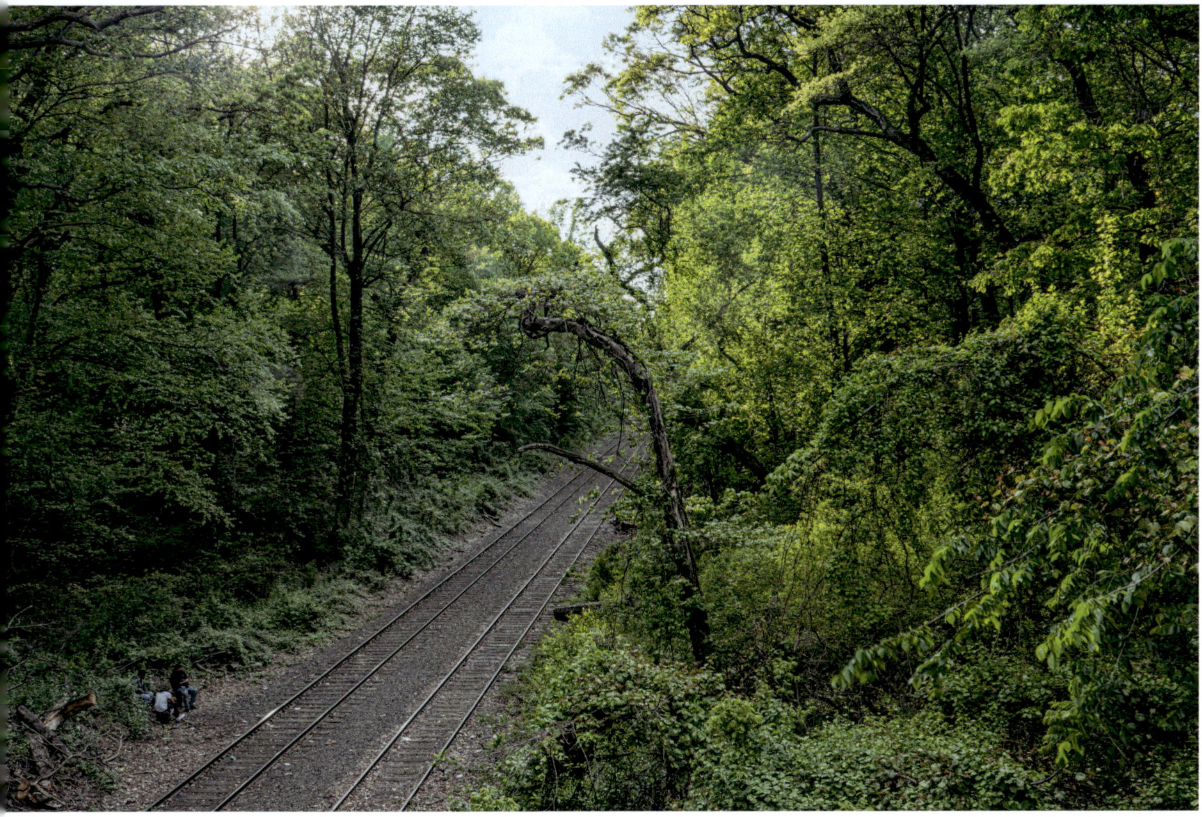

Is the best of all possible worlds as good as you expected it to be?

Kommen diese beiden Hälften — das Individuum und die Stadt, Text und Bild — zu einem Ganzen zusammen? Natürlich nicht. Was ist von einer Stadtsymphonie in einer immerwährenden Wirtschaftskrise und einem Mea culpa einer Person, die nur durch Prämissen existiert, zu halten? «Alltag als Sinn der Parteilichkeit in der Mimesis» war Lukács' Slogan für den Realismus, was diese Arbeit nicht sein kann oder zu sein versagt. Auch entspricht sie nicht den strengen Kriterien der überparteilichen ästhetischen Autonomie, deren Absolution im Kalten Krieg gegen die instrumentelle Vernunft (siehe Adorno und Marcuse versus Lukács) wie die Beute eines Pyrrhussieges in der Gegenwart nachhallt. Abgesehen von dem Vorwurf des Dilettantismus, der zum Teil auf den offensichtlichen Mangel an Engagement oder Ernsthaftigkeit zurückzuführen ist, wäre es von Vorteil, eine künstlerische Strategie vorzuschlagen, die weder die spontane künstlerisch-aktivistische Philosophie noch die unmittelbaren Ergebnisse des Prozesses der ästhetischen Autonomie vermittelt? Du bist verdammt, wenn du es tust, und du bist verdammt, wenn du es nicht tust? Wenn es besser wäre, auf noble Weise zu scheitern, als auf niederträchtige Weise erfolgreich zu sein, würde dann das Scheitern einer Gesellschaftsform die Möglichkeit einer anderen eröffnen? Der Versuch dieser Arbeit, den unüberwindbaren Gegensatz ungleicher Teile — Individuum und Gesellschaft — zu artikulieren, ist eine Wette, dass eine solche Opposition umso prägnanter erscheint, desto mehr sie sich bemüht, alltäglich zu wirken. Dies ist keineswegs ein Ansatz, eine selbstgefällige Verzweiflung vorzutäuschen. Individuen sind nur dann mit dem gleichen Massstab messbar, wenn sie unter einem einzigen Gesichtspunkt betrachtet werden. Wenn ein abstraktes Individuum als machtlos überdeterminiert würde, wäre sein Fehlen an gesellschaftlicher Handlungsfähigkeit demonstrativ. Die einzige wirkliche Möglichkeit in der Gesellschaft — in konkreter Kollektivität — würde nur durch eine Einladung zur kritischen Negation erkannt werden.

Wenn sich jemand die Zeit nehmen würde, eine der gestellten Fragen dieses Buches zu beantworten, dann bezweifle ich, dass die Antwort dieser Person mit der Antwort derjenigen Person übereinstimmt, die sie

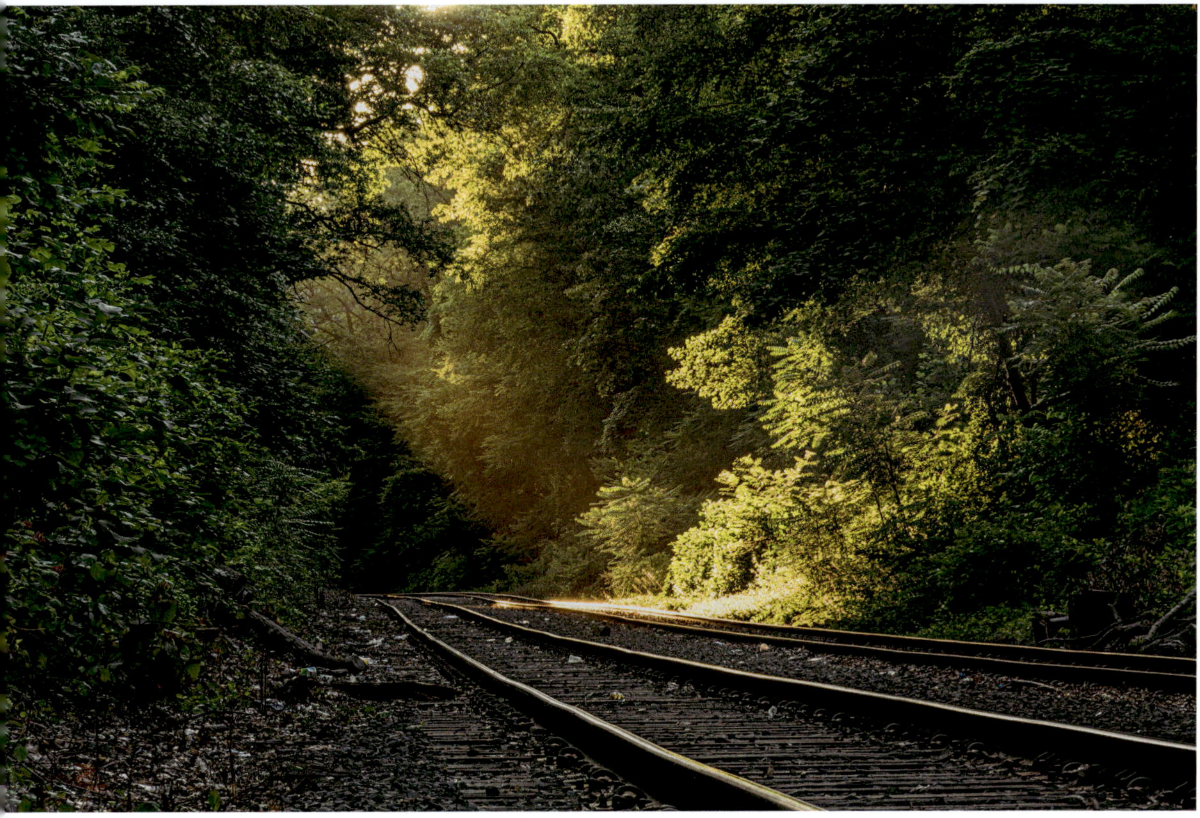

If there were no endings, would it be a relief to not have to fret over a good one?

unterwirft und deren Bedürfnisse bisher das Interesse als solches definiert hat.

ANMERKUNGEN

(1) Jean-Jacques Rousseau, *Émile oder Über die Erziehung* (1762), übersetzt von Hermann Denhardt (Berlin: Edition Deutsche Klassik GmbH, 2013), 8.

(2) Aus dem Englischen: Thorstein Veblen, *The Theory of Business Enterprise* (1904), ed. Douglas Dowd (New Brunswick, NJ: Transaction Books, 1978), 241.

(3) Paul Samuelson, *Volkswirtschaftslehre: Das internationale Standardwerk der Makro- und Mikroökonomie* (1948), übersetzt von William D. Nordhaus (München: FBV, 2017), 38.

(4) Das ist eine paraphrasierte Version von: Robert Brenner, «Escalating Plunder», *New Left Review*, 123, Mai/Juni 2020.

(5) Ernst Bloch, "Karl Marx und die Menschlichkeit: Stoff der Hoffnung" (1969), in: *Das Prinzip Hoffnung* (Frankfurt: Suhrkamp, 1976), 43-44.

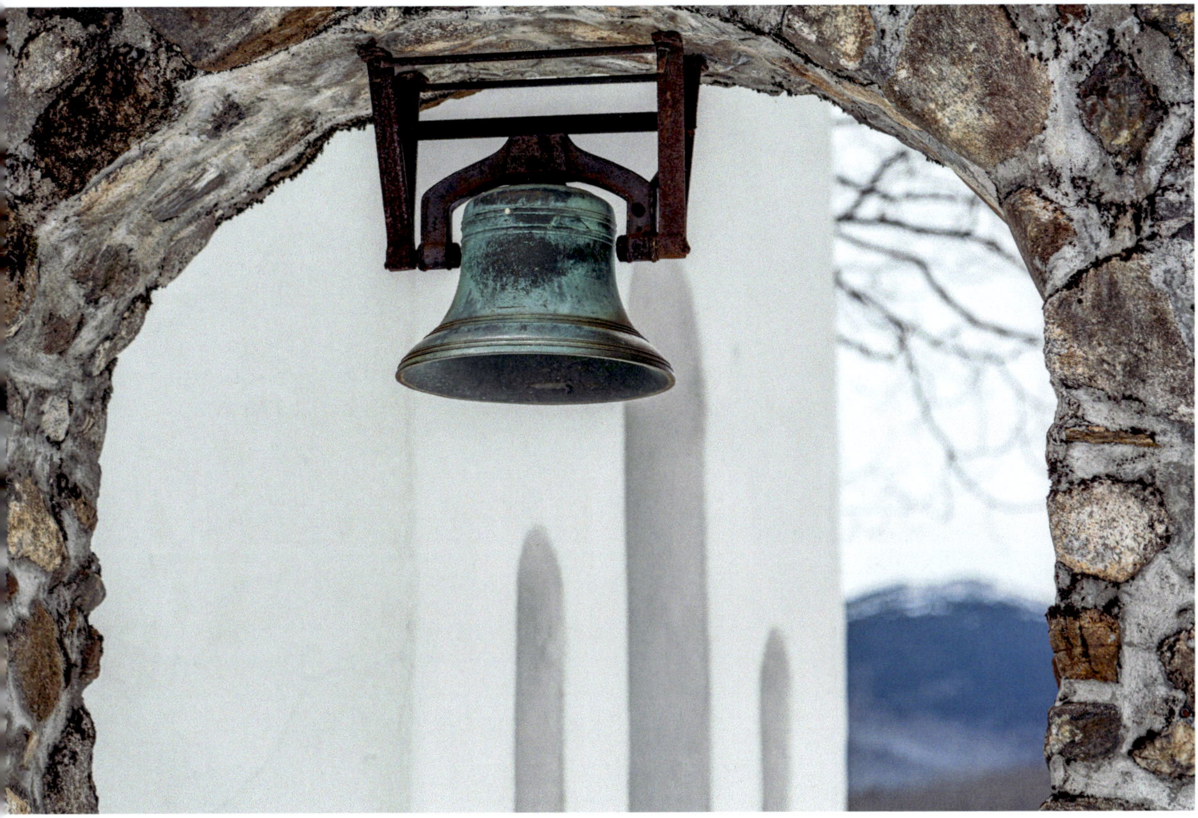

Will never enough make do?

Index

31 *City Acres*
Kannst du einem Kind erklären, wie du deinen Lebensunterhalt verdienst?

33 *Point Breeze*
Wartest du auf einen Moment, der einfach nicht kommen will?

35 *Douglass St*
Wartest du auf einen Moment, der bereits gekommen ist?

37 *Allen St*
Kannst du profitieren, wenn du die Extraktionsbedingungen beseitigst?

39 *Rulers Bar Hassock*
Hast du dich entschieden, nicht das Leben zu leben, in das du hineingeboren wurdest?

41 *"Spatial Fix"—for kids*
Wirst du stets der Entfernung begegnen, von der aus du gestartet bist?

43 *East River*
Identifizierst du dich mit der Person, als die du erinnert wirst?

45 *Nassau St*
Wenn es nicht genug von allem gibt, ist dann nichts genug?

47 *Krikko's Midtown*
Kannst du deinen Kopf so tief in den Sand stecken, dass er auf der anderen Seite hervorspriesst?

49 *Maiden Ln*
Ist es eine Katastrophe, wenn es gewöhnlich ist?

51 *Recovery to Resiliency, Pearl St*
Zählt dein Verlangen?

53 *Summit St*
Hast du das am Hals, was du nicht hast?

55 *Hudson Yards*
Sind deine Sinne an eine Form gebunden, die an einer anderen Stelle Schmerzen auslöst?

109 *Flushing Ave*
Stehst du unter Gleichen an der Spitze?

111 *West St*
Ist ein Leben ohne Abenteuer nicht lebenswert?

113 *King St*
Ist dein Wohlergehen der Nettoprofit von jemand anderem?

115 *Schermerhorn St*
Warst du mal die Ausrede für die Grausamkeit von jemand anderem?

117 *Crookes Point*
Sind deine Hoffnungen das Vermächtnis von jemand anderem?

119 *2016–2019*
Nimmst du einen gewissen Verlust in Kauf, um an einer anderen Stelle Gewinn zu erzielen?

121 *The New York & Atlantic Railway, Forest Park (I)*
Ist die beste aller möglichen Welten so gut, wie du es erwartet hast?

123 *The New York & Atlantic Railway, Forest Park (II)*
Wenn es kein Ende gäbe, wäre es dann eine Erleichterung, sich nicht um ein gutes Ende sorgen zu müssen?

125 *At the foot of the lighthouse is no light – Ernst Bloch, Stone Pond, NH*
Wird nie genug reichen?

The Premise of a Better Life is a multi-part artwork from 2019. Except for the works on pages 57, 59, 63 and 65, which are UV-prints on PVC with UV-printed acrylic glass, all works are C-Prints with UV-printed acrylic glass. The measurement of each work is 59.4 x 84.1 cm.

The Premise of a Better Life (2019) ist ein mehrteiliges Kunstwerk, das erstmals im Kunsthaus Glarus gezeigt wurde. Alle Arbeiten sind C-Prints unter UV-bedrucktem Acrylglas mit Ausnahme derjenigen auf den Seiten 57, 59, 63 und 65, die UV-Drucke auf PVC unter UV-bedrucktem Acrylglas sind. Die Masse jedes Werkes sind 59,4 x 84,1 cm.

This book is published following the exhibition /
Diese Publikation erscheint anlässlich der Ausstellung:

Sam Pulitzer
The Premise of a Better Life
Kunsthaus Glarus
Oct. 27, 2019 — Jan. 1st, 2020.

The exhibition and the publication were generously supported by /
Die Ausstellung und die Publikation wurden unterstützt von:
Stiftung der Glarner Kantonalbank für ein starkes Glarnerland,
Dr. Georg & Josi Guggenheim Stiftung, Migros-Kulturprozent,
Swisslos Kulturfonds Kanton Glarus, Stiftung Anne-Marie Schindler,
Sandoz Fondation de Famille, Galerie Francesca Pia,
Galerie Lars Friedrich

Published by / Erschienen im: After 8 Books, Paris
www.after8books.com

Editor / Herausgeber: Judith Welter / Kunsthaus Glarus
Management / Verwaltung: Benjamin Thorel
Translation / Übersetzung: Michèle Graf, Selina Grüter
Copyediting / Lektorat und Korrektorat:
Stefanie Baehr, Julian Reidy, Judith Welter
Design / Gestaltung: Sabo Day
Lithography / Lithographie: MaxColor
Printed in Germany by / Gedruckt in Deutschland von:
DZA Druckerei zu Altenburg GmBH

Distribution / Vertrieb:
France & Belgique: Interart, Paris, www.interart.fr
United Kingdom: Art Data, London, www.artdata.co.uk
The Americas, Asia, and Australia:
DAP | Distributed Art Publishers, New York, www.artbook.com

Thanks to / Dank an: Marie Karlberg, Bill Hayden,
Ben Morgan-Cleveland, Annie Ochmanek, Caleb Considine,
Francesca Pia, Leo Lencsés, Lars Friedrich, Inka Meissner,
Fernando Mesta, José Rojas

This book is the fourth in the singles series from After 8 Books

ISBN: 9782492650024
Dépôt légal: Mars 2022

After 8 Books

Louis-Auguste Blanqui,
Eternity by the Stars (1872), tr. Frank Chouraqui
(New York & Berlin: Contra Mundum Press, 2013)

C. P. Cavafy,
"The City" (1911), in *The Complete Poems of Cavafy*,
tr. Rae Delvin
(New York: Harcourt, Brace & World, 1961)